THE METAPHOR OF SHEPHERD IN THE HEBREW BIBLE

A Historical-Literary Reading

Jonathan Gan

University Press of America,® Inc.
Lanham · Boulder · New York · Toronto · Plymouth, UK

Copyright © 2007 by
University Press of America,® Inc.
4501 Forbes Boulevard
Suite 200
Lanham, Maryland 20706
UPA Acquisitions Department (301) 459-3366

Estover Road
Plymouth PL6 7PY
United Kingdom

Library of Congress Control Number: 2007928760
ISBN-13: 978-0-7618-3754-1 (paperback : alk. paper)
ISBN-10: 0-7618-3754-X (paperback : alk. paper)

To

the LORD

and

my wife, Lucinda

CONTENTS

PREFACE

One of the most important theological imagery in the Hebrew Bible is the metaphor of shepherd. Many books on pastoral theology had written about the topic, but they were presented with a different orientation. The contemporary image of shepherd inclines toward a therapist, counselor, and care-giver. However, careful study of the metaphor in the Hebrew Bible proves otherwise.

This book presupposes that the metaphor of shepherd begins with Yahweh is significant to the New Testament meaning of the image and may be the basis for the study of the metaphor in the Bible. Studies of the shepherd image in the New Testament must relate to the shepherd metaphor in the Hebrew Bible. It is through the Hebrew Bible that this image of shepherd is understood in greater depths and in relation to the Israelite nation.

The book is designed to reveal the all original meanings, possibly, of shepherd image in the Hebrew Bible. The metaphor of shepherd is expressed not only in Yahweh, but also in various biblical characters such as Abraham, Moses, David, and so forth. However, the focus is not on the person designated as shepherd. Rather, the attention is on the roles and characteristics of a shepherd that were manifested in the biblical characters or offices through the texts.

The approach in this study is historical-literary by sifting through the Hebrew Bible. Meaning is not derived through theological traditions, rather through exegesis in the historical and literary contexts expressed through those written words. Also, it does not confine to interpretation within a particular theological traditions. Every major section of the Hebrew Bible will be examined. To achieve this end, the process of study follows the divisions of the Jewish Canon; the Torah, the Prophets, and the Writings.

The book concludes with the implications of the shepherd metaphor to biblical studies. It is desired to draw the attention to the biblical meaning of shepherd, beginning with the Hebrew Bible, and to unplug from a distorted perspective. It is believed that there is a place for the biblical image of shepherd as in the Hebrew Bible in the contemporary biblical studies.

In the process of writing, I must give appreciation to the resourceful libraries that enable this research. They are Trinity Western University, Langley, Regent College; Tyndale University College (formerly Tyndale College and Seminary); and Trinity Theological College (Singapore). Especially, Trinity Western University, the library contains critical materials for the writings of this book. I also want to thank Dr. Paul Kruger, Associate Professor of Ancient Studies, Stellenbosch Univesity, and Dr. Hans van Deventer, Senior Lecturer in Biblical Studies (Old Testament), North-West University (formerly Potchefstroom University, South Africa) for their brief interaction and support. Lastly, I want to thank my wife, Lucinda, who has been patiently making this research possible, and forbear with the agony of the writing process. I would like to offer this book to any interested readers and serious students of the Hebrew Bible, and hope to encourage more research in motion. Most of all, to God be the glory.

Jonathan Gan
Vancouver, Canada
25 March, 2005

ABBREVIATIONS

Hebrew Bible/Old Testament

Genesis	Ge	Ecclesiastes	Ecc
Exodus	Ex	Song of Songs	SS
Leviticus	Lev	Isaiah	Isa
Numbers	Nu	Jeremiah	Jer
Deuteronomy	Dt	Lamentations	La
Joshua	Jos	Ezekiel	Eze
Judges	Jdg	Daniel	Da
Ruth	Ru	Hosea	Hos
1 Samuel	1 Sa	Joel	Joel
2 Samuel	2 Sa	Amos	Am
1 Kings	1 Ki	Obadiah	Ob
2 Kings	2 Ki	Jonah	Jnh
1 Chronicles	1 Ch	Micah	Mic
2 Chronicles	2 Ch	Nahum	Na
Ezra	Ezr	Habakkuk	Hab
Nehemiah	Ne	Zephaniah	Zep
Esther	Est	Haggai	Hag
Job	Job	Zechariah	Zec
Psalms	Ps	Malachi	Mal
Proverbs	Pr		

New Testament

Matthew	Mt	1 Timothy	1 Ti
Mark	Mk	2 Timothy	2 Ti
Luke	Lk	Titus	Tit
John	Jn	Philemon	Phm
Acts	Ac	Hebrews	Heb
Romans	Ro	James	Jas
1 Corinthians	1 Co	1 Peter	1 Pe
2 Corinthians	2 Co	2 Peter	2 Pe
Galatians	Gal	1 John	1 Jn
Ephesians	Eph	2 John	2 Jn
Philippians	Php	3 John	3 Jn
Colossians	Col	Jude	Jude
1 Thessalonians	1 Th	Revelation	Rev
2 Thessalonians	2 Th		

INTRODUCTION

The metaphor of shepherd is the prominent metaphor used in defining the pastoral role in the church throughout centuries. It can be seen as a component of the practical skills that a pastor should have to manage church ministry in the contemporary world.

Some pastors seem to work professionally in their pastoral duties with the application of social science theories (Tidball 1986, 13). With the help of the human sciences, pastoral ministry seems to come to life, especially, with the application of management principles. These techniques make pastors feel adequate to minister and to lead the church. The contributions of the social sciences and management principles have been toward practical skills that equipped pastors with these techniques, however without sound biblical foundation.

The usage of the metaphor of shepherd in pastoral ministry has deviated at a slight degree from the picture of God as shepherd in the Hebrew Bible. The shepherd metaphor often relates to the New Testament model of shepherd, occasionally to God as shepherd in Psalm 23. In so doing, the shepherd metaphor has a therapeutic effect on the people ministered, due to the concept of shepherd dependent on New Testament theology (see Tidball 1986). But the picture is incomplete without the counterparts of the Hebrew Bible that portrays God as a shepherd in a way beyond the therapeutic image.

The Hebrew Bible depicts the metaphor of shepherd diversely in God, Abraham, Moses, David, and others. This rich manifestation of the metaphor of shepherd becomes a source of reference to the study of the shepherd metaphor in the biblical text. It is to this purpose that this book humbly attempts to excavate the neglected aspects of the shepherd metaphor in the Hebrew biblical materials, so that one can grasp the full meaning of this important biblical metaphor. It is not in any way an exhaustive and conclusive study of the shepherd metaphor, but a preliminary exploration of the shepherd figure in the Hebrew Bible.

The way to conduct this study is through historical-literary exegesis approach to the study of metaphor in the Hebrew Bible. Historical-literary exegesis embraces many critical methods in its application, and thus may derive a sensible interpretation of the text. Literary and linguistic skills such as genre criticism, grammars and sentence structures are essential knowledge to interpretation, but must be read within the historical context to determine the meaning more comprehensively. History provides the big picture and literary theory enlightens the details.

This book does not necessary target to academics, but also students and all those who are interested in this topic. The style of writing is served to embrace this objective, so that readers may travel at ease through the unfamiliar field, and may benefit their understanding of the topic and its approach. In addition, the sections of the Hebrew Bible in this study have been arranged according to the Hebrew Bible canonical order.

CHAPTER ONE

THE METAPHOR OF SHEPHERD
IN PASTORAL THEOLOGY

Pastoral theology relies much on the metaphor of shepherd lacks the under-standing of the metaphor in the Hebrew Bible, which is essential to the subject. To understand the shepherd metaphor depicted in the Hebrew Bible, one must inquire the use of shepherd metaphor in the formation of pastoral theology in the research process. The following will help us to understand the deficiency of the shepherd metaphor presented in pastoral theology.

The implementation of social sciences and management theories, though in a sense has revived pastoral work from being overtly practical, still lacks solid theological element which the pastoral ministry should lay its foundation. The changes brought about by the social sciences and management principles, are insufficient to give pastors, a sense of direction for the spiritual work that is grounded on theological foundations.

David Fisher (1996) described the pastoral ministry as being tougher than it has ever been before. He said that, "the world is experiencing rapid and perpet-ual change" (Fisher 1996, 7). Fisher continued to state that there is a lapse of theology in pastoral ministry. The modern perception of pastoral ministry is such that, "the practice of ministry has become the theology" (Fisher 1996, 9). The pastoral role has changed to become the model. Theology and practice have reversed their roles, and this can be seen in the history of the Christian ministry.

Historically, pastoral theology used to be the core of pastoral studies in the theological education curriculum. But, in this century, practical theology has become the prominent feature of pastoral studies. Practical theology refers to the practical application of theology, that which embraces subjects such as religious education, missiology, pastoral therapy, and other empirical oriented subjects. It turns pastoral education into practical application of theology in ministry, rather than being governed and reflected upon by theology. Phenomena in pastoral practice have changed and it is critical for us to reflect upon them.

Six Phenomena of Pastoral Theology

In our study of pastoral theology, there are six phenomena presented by Derek J. Tidball (1986) that must be considered. These phenomena, though have been presented about two decades ago, it is still relevant to our present pastoral situation. Pastoral image or figure does not change through times as much as it should, since World-War II. Many of the images in the pre-war era have been retained in the mind of the pastors themselves, as well as in the congregation. In order to effect changes in pastoral theology for the new era, it is critical to reflect on the phenomena clustering the pastoral image.

Firstly, the pastoral role as shepherd has been undervalued. Anthony Russell (1980, 262) said, to this regard that, "at all levels in the Church there is an awareness that the ministry is passing through not just a period of temporary uncertainty but a profound crisis." The shepherd is now in a marginal position in some countries and societies with skills, expertise and perspectives that "have no market value" (Russell 1980, 281–282). Yet, the role of the pastor is still based on some agrarian cultural ideologies of shepherd skills and perspectives.

Secondly, the metaphor of shepherd was outmoded (see Isa 40:11). The terms "sheep" and "shepherds" are estranged to the people of modern and non-agricultural society. The biblical analogy of the relationship between the shepherd and sheep conveys a message that is alienated from the modern cultural setting (Tidball 1986, 15). There is no assimilated experience of shepherd metaphor in the modern mind. But the twentieth–first century pastoral theology still heavily anchored on the image of shepherd that belongs to an agrarian culture.

Thirdly, the setting regarding pastoral role in the church has shifted and was no longer the same. The effects of the Industrial Revolution created tensions on pastoral responsibilities towards the community; especially, when faced with the shifts of population from rural to urban areas, the traditional pastoral role became difficult in ministering to peoples' needs. Although lifestyle has changed, the practice of pastoral ministry remains unchanged to the hectic lifestyle of the urban city, and that is disconnected to the real world.

Fourthly, research on pastoral office has become prominent. Changes have taken place in church structures, especially those outside the mainstream denomination churches. The effects of change, however, have also encouraged the mainstream denominations to rethink the functions and roles of the pastor (Tidball 1986, 16). It is critical for pastoral theologian to revisit the discipline of pastoral theology in relation to the development of the contemporary church, and to reflect the role of the pastor as shepherd in the new era of church history.

Fifthly, with the alienation of the shepherd metaphor to the present culture, the traditional approach to pastoral ministry has become "old-fashioned" (Tidball 1986, 16). If this is the understanding of pastoral theology, the Christian truths applied in pastoral practice increase the question of its validity (Tidball 1986, 17). To this regard, Tidball (1986, 17) brought to our attention an obligatory responsibility of pastoral theology in the provision of a quality life nurturing process. Perhaps, the metaphor of shepherd, according to Tidball, is best understood as the re-shaping of perspective in life, rather than the tending of sheep. In other words, the pastor is to guide his flock as a spiritual director in living the Christian life.

Sixthly, the form of pastoral roles appeared to be ambiguous. On this, Tidball (1986) added that at a glance, it appears to be the restoration of creation. At the extreme, the distinction between the church and world is removed, and the outcome is a reversed leadership; the world leads the church, not the reverse (Tidball 1986, 17). The changes in the present society have made the pastoral role unfitting. Pastoral theology must find a new identity in the modern society. It is also the right time to rethink about pastoral theology and for theological colleges to reflect upon their pastoral studies curriculum.

Definition Revisit

Before going further, it is important to clarify the meaning of pastoral theology. Without a clear understanding of what is pastoral theology, efforts to examine church-related ministries through pastoral theological perspectives will be futile. Defining pastoral theology will help us to identify the relationship between pastoral theology and church-related ministries, which embrace subjects such as worship, evangelism, Sunday School, and missions.

Thomas C. Oden

What then is pastoral theology? Defining pastoral theology has been difficult throughout the history of the Christian ministry. Many attempts have been made to obtain a comprehensive definition that is conducive to embrace all aspects of pastoral theology, true to its term. Thomas C. Oden (1983, x) defined pastoral theology as, "that branch of Christian theology that deals with the office and functions of the pastor." This definition is somewhat confusing. It is a reflection of multiple elements. The involvement from tradition, critical reasoning, to personal and social experiences is challenging (Oden 1983, 311).

The definition of Oden is excellent, yet lacks a complete evaluation of pastoral theology. The idea of Oden is closely linked to the ordained ministry and to its functions. This definition works well only in the older days of pastoral ministry when church life was not so complex. Contemporary churches have more roles played by the laity. Ministries such as small groups does not depend on the pastor, ordained or not.[1] Laity involvement is of paramount importance to the success of small group ministry. The role of the pastor must be conspicuous. Thus, it is necessary to rethinking pastoral theology.

Martin Thornton

The definition of pastoral theology by Martin Thornton (1956, 6) outlined that, "ascetical theology, with moral theology as its correlate, is the true core of pastoral practice." Thornton perceived ascetical theology and moral theology as headed by the subject of pastoral theology. He also urges that the definition must be precise.

The definition offered by Thornton needs a clearer definition. Subsequently, Thornton (1968) reviewed this definition, and offered a more precise one. He defines pastoral theology as an, "adaptation of doctrine by the pastor in the general oversight of the flock" and what has been previously stated to be the "core of pastoral practice" was now labeled "applied or ascetical theology" (Thornton 1968, 37).

The later definition by Thornton (1968, 37) seems to be a clearer definition of pastoral theology. It heightens the perspective of pastoral theology and brings into focus that it is to be the application of the doctrine that seems fit by the pastor to be used for the spiritual benefit of the congregation. It also surfaces the notion of pastoral sensitivity in the practice of Christian ministry. However, his emphasis is implicitly centered upon the spirituality of the pastor.

Pastoral theology, etymologically, has to involve pastoral ministry, the pastor, and theology. Spirituality without ministry will elevate pride and become irrelevant to the earthly matters. Besides, spirituality is too personal to benefit anybody, significantly. Therefore, a good pastoral theology must balance pastoral practice and the person, with theology. Thornton (1968) failed to develop such balance in his definition of pastoral theology, revision has been done. Thus, it is necessary to rethinking pastoral theology.

Seward Hiltner

According to Seward Hiltner (1958, 20), pastoral theology is,

> that branch or field of theological knowledge and inquiry that brings the shepherding perspective to bear upon all the operations and functions of the church and minister, and then draws conclusions of a theological order from reflection on these observation.

Hiltner's definition has three helpful elements. First, pastoral theology cannot be defined within the confine of one aspect of the Christian ministry, but rather by the macro-perspective of the entire pastoral ministry. Second, pastoral theology is a branch of theology in its true sense, as any branch of theology. Third, it emphasizes the relationship between theology and pastoral tasks, so that pastoral ministry finds its base in theology, for the practice of Christian ministry.

This definition, however, is also confined to offices and functions of the church; Christian ministry and the pastor, similar to that of Oden. The definition provided by Hiltner is subjective, if analyzed with the term pastoral and theology. "Theological order" here, refers to the practice of Christian ministry. Formulating "theological order" from the observation of the operations and functions of the church ministry may fail to have an objective and comprehensive perspective of the pastoral role, and juxtapose pastoral theology in subjection to personal and subjective opinions (see Tit 2:1). Pastoral practices should be guarded and guided by biblical theological perspective. It is the role of the pastor to reflect Christian ministry and pastoral practices through theology derived from the exegesis of the Bible. The term "theological order" is too vague in Hiltner's definition, and subject to the sway of denominational stance. To foster "theological order" as in practices of Christian ministry from the observation of the operations and functions of the church ministry is drifting away from the theological foundations of pastoral theology. Hitlner's definition needs fine tuning. Thus, it is necessary to rethinking pastoral theology.

Carl Kromminga

Carl Kromminga raised his objection to the terminology employed by Hiltner in his definition, which tended to categorize pastoral theology as a functional discipline. He outlined that the definition of Hiltner has a functional approach that hinders the discipline at the theological level. Pastoral theology is limited by the fact that functional operations and theology are dichotomized; theology cannot define pastoral practice, and theology is the foundation of pastoral practice. It does not satisfy the theological search and solution to pastoral practice.[2]

By limiting the theological expansion of the discipline, it disqualifies being pastoral theology. Theology cannot and must not derive solely from the operations and functions of church ministry. Otherwise, the theology that formulates "theological order" will fall prey to relativism. If that is true, pastoral theology will eventually become relative to the work of the church ministry, rather than the theological understanding of the pastoral assignment given and endorsed by God with a special setting apart. However, Kromminga's definition has the similar subjectivity as Hiltner. If theology is derived from the observation of church ministry operations, opinionated theology may be formulated. Thus, Kromminga has not clearly defined pastoral theology and required rethinking.

William G.T. Shedd

Other contribution to the definition of pastoral theology came from William G.T. Shedd (1965, 320) who defined a pastor as one that, "requires the special discipline that qualifies him to watch over the personal religious interests of his flock." Shedd (1965, 320) also stressed that pastoral theology should be the theological curriculum catered for the clergyman's life. Simply put, pastoral theology may be the theology of pastoral life.

Such definition is too simplistic. If pastoral theology is the theology of pastoral life, it should be called pastoral spiritual theology. But pastoral theology is more than simply concerning the theology of pastoral life, it also concerned about the role of the pastor in relation to the church ministry. Theology should define pastoral practice and in return review theology for church ministry. Again, this definition falls short of a comprehensive definition of pastoral theology, and thus needs rethinking.

John C. Thiessen

John C. Thiessen dealt with the subject of pastoral theology in an epistemological manner. To Thiessen (1962, 13), the term, "pastoral", undeniably related to the work of a minister, and the term, "theology", related to God and the scripture. So, pastoral theology, according to Thiessen, is related to the pastoral work and Scripture. This is similar to Oden's definition, and of course, has the similar shortfalls. The definition of Thiessen is not comprehensive to embrace all meanings of the term. Like Oden, Thiessen's definition is related to pastoral office and function, which suited only for agrarian society and specifically ordained ministry. Unlike Oden, Thiessen's definition of pastoral theology is not elucidated, and thus it is not comprehensive to define the subject. Thus, it is necessary to rethinking pastoral theology.

Jay E. Adams

Jay E. Adams (1979) outlined the real problem of the pastor failing to minister. It is not that of ability or capability, but rather the, "shoddy or erroneous Biblical understanding or theological thinking" (Adams 1979, 2). Adams (1979, 3) further said that the integration of exegesis and theology in pastoral practice must accompany by wisdom and aptitude that which required in church ministry.

Ministry skill is necessary for pastoral operations. In this respect, pastoral theology may be seen in relation to pastoral care. At this point, the definition of pastoral theology is not explained clearly. Thus, it is necessary to rethinking pastoral theology. The relationship between pastoral theology and pastoral care is discussed in the next definition.

William A. Clebsch and Charles R. Jaekle

William A. Clebsch and Charles R. Jaekle (1964, 8–10) perceived pastoral theology in relation to the cure of souls or pastoral care. In this case, it consisted of four functions such as, healing, sustaining, guiding and reconciling.

Both Adams (1979) and Clebsch and Jaekle (1964) relate pastoral theology to humanistic or therapeutic ideology. The focus is on the functional and operational capacities of the pastor, rather than the theological foundations of the shepherding role. This is somewhat similar to Oden's (1983) definition. Pastoral theology in this mode will suffer under subjective perspective or opinionated theology, which may not perform as the guide to pastoral practice. Thus, re-thinking of pastoral theology is necessary.

Derek J. Tidball

The most satisfactory definition of pastoral theology as far as theological and pastoral meaning of the term is concerned, is that of Derek J. Tidball (1986). His definition is somewhat similar to that of Hiltner (1958) but beyond the confines of church ministry and pastor. There is a difference in perspectives of theology and pastoral experience between Tidball and Hiltner. Hiltner emphasized pastoral theology with reference to church, ministry and the pastor. To Tidball, theology is translated by shepherding perspective. It informs and reflects on theology, and in return, the theology informs and reflects on the pastoral work, which is an irreversible relationship (Tidball 1986, 24).

The definition of Tidball (1986) contains the essential of the term pastoral theology in that the emphasis is on theology, not on pastoral experience and ministry, or reflection based on church ministry experiences. As Hiltner (1958) also suggested, while these ideas appeared to be inevitably related, pastoral experience should not be examined by itself, but by the theological framework that derived from biblical sources. Having theology as the foundation, pastoral ministry can be refined and reflected theologically to the spiritual benefits of the congregation. The failure Hiltner had in his definition is the emphasis of a "theological order," in which inclines too much to ministry experiences, rather than theology. Tidball's definition has propounded the idea of theological foundation as the prerequisite to the formulation of pastoral theology.

What Tidball (1986) must emphasize is how theology derives from the biblical materials and shepherding perspective derives from biblical exegesis. In other words, pastoral theology must be formulated from sound biblical theology that which derives from the biblical understanding of the metaphor of shepherd.

Pastoral Theology and
Other Theological Disciplines

The relationship of pastoral care with pastoral theology is vicarious. As discussed earlier, pastoral theology has its emphasis on theology, rather than the church ministry experiences. If pastoral care is dealing with the manner of practical acts in church ministry, it cannot be a part of pastoral theology. However, if the discussion revolves around the theological theory of pastoral care, then it can be established as a part of the pastoral theology discipline. Thus, the relationship is implicit, rather than explicit.

Practical theology is another discipline closely related to pastoral theology. In some continents, pastoral theology forms part of practical theological studies. But pastoral theology differs from practical theology in that the former deals with theology "seen" from a pastoral or shepherding perspective, while the latter deals with the practical applications of theology. Besides, applying theology into church ministry must take alignment from the shepherding perspective, not from the observation of operational experiences. Practical theology is also distinct from pastoral care, except in the discussions of empirical theory of pastoral care. So, pastoral theology is the heart of practical theology and is a discipline which relates both theology and practice of church ministry, and the pastoral role. It could be argued that pastoral theology is the means to bridge practices derive from the theological foundations and shepherding characteristics. Pastoral theology is, just as Tidball (1986, 34) stated, "theology seen from shepherding perspective."

What is observed thus far is that there is a shortfall of the understanding of the biblical picture of shepherd. The third area in relation to pastoral theology is biblical theology. The common derivation of shepherd metaphor comes from church oriented and functional operative perspectives. It should stem from the shepherd metaphor in the Bible, instead. Shepherd metaphor must be understood prior to the formulation of pastoral theology and its implications to church-related ministries. As argued earlier, the picture of shepherd in the Hebrew Bible should be the foundation of the metaphor of shepherd that which the New Testament and pastoral theology should anchor.

To achieve this end, we must first establish an approach to the topic of shepherd metaphor. To this, now we turn to the hermeneutical methodology.

Notes

1. The term "small groups" refers to pockets of people gathered in the format of a group for Bible studies, prayers, and pastoral care. Sometimes, it is also known in other names such as "cell groups", "care groups", "life groups", and so forth. But Ralph Neighbors (1990) understood cell group differently and has formulated an alternative format which is popular in some parts of North America and Singapore.

2. Cited by Tidball 1986, 23, from the Introduction to S. Volbeda, *The Pastoral Genius of Preaching*, n. p.; see also Anderson (1979, 7).

CHAPTER TWO

THE HERMENEUTICAL METHODOLOGY

The study of metaphor requires a methodology that is appropriate to the nature of the subject. Unlike narratives and prophecies in the Hebrew Bible, the study of metaphor requires the examination of all genres, rather than limited to a particular literary type. This chapter aims to deal with the methodology used in the study of metaphor. It does not attempt to be a comprehensive critique to all critical methods to the study of the Hebrew Bible, rather in search of an appropriate way to do the topic of shepherd metaphor. Furthermore, exegesis and interpretation must be accompanied with theological objectives. The study of metaphor is not simply a linguistic exercise, or doctrinal proof-text. It involves the study of language, concept, context, and theological ideas.

To determine a right method to the study of metaphor is difficult. However, it is critical to form one. This chapter will establish a method that would be used in the study of the metaphor of shepherd for the rest of the book. Since the emergence of the Biblical Theology Movement and metaphor conveys theological ideology, discussions regarding the right approaches to this discipline are enormous. Yet, no one method seems to be the best. This section aims to review some of these approaches to observe why these methods are not appropriate to the study of the subject metaphor. The end-result is to suggest an approach of exegesis that is viable to this subject.

Diachronic Method

The diachronic method is championed by the renowned German scholar, Gerhard von Rad (1975). This method is based on the historical unfolding of the events in the ancient Israel. Von Rad believed that such interpretation of historical events must align with the traditions of the historic Israel. He stated that the integration of traditions and theology in historical exegesis must have preference over the combination of intellectual and theology (Rad 1975, 116). The result of the process generates outdated traditions that alienate themselves from the original meaning. The only way to connect these foreign traditions to the life of Israel is to relate these traditions in light of the entirety of Israel nation, socially, politically, and religiously (Rad 1975, 118).

The faith of Israel builds on the foundational events in their history (Rad 1975, 120). Von Rad added that it is detrimental to the historical narratives of Israel if our understanding is based on theological categories. He asserted that re-telling the stories of the Hebrew Bible is the right form of theological discourse (Rad 1975, 121). But this approach is arbitrary. Re-telling or reconstructing historical events can be a dangerous game. Bias and theological stances often direct the way we interpret the events, and that is why scholars differ in interpretation of the same text. Traditions are useful as a reference guide but at the same time, we must be sensitive to the changes that take place in the sociological, economic, and political spheres. These factors affect the meaning we perceived in the text. They contribute to the significance of the event to the nation of Israel and the Diaspora. Without which, interpretation becomes a detached piece of work finding no place in history and culture of the ancient Israel.

The biblical text is the critical piece of information for appropriate interpretation. In the study of metaphor, exegetical and literary skills are essentially required. It is critical to excavate exegetically the pattern and concept exhibited in the text to enlighten our understanding of its meaning in the ancient biblical manuscripts. Theology that is hidden in the metaphor must be derived from the text, rather than from theological concepts. The meaning of metaphor comes from the exegesis of the biblical text, allowing the written material to paint the image of shepherd in the ancient world. It is not simply by retelling the story of crossing the Red Sea that explains the meaning of Yahweh's power, but the observing of the discourse and consulting the historical event that portrays the majestic power of Yahweh. Therefore, diachronic approach, in von Rad's terms, which is heavily based on tradition criticism and lacks sensitivity in literary and historical contexts, is inappropriate for the study of metaphor.

Thematic Method

The thematic approach advocated by Walther Eichrodt (1961) is based on the theme of covenant, as in opposition to the historical approach in the study of the Hebrew Bible. The purpose is to recover the proper understanding of the Hebrew Bible from the influence of historicism. Eichrodt (1961) stated that historical approach to the Hebrew Bible should be discarded and a new approach should be discovered. The crisis in biblical studies, according to Eichrodt, is the textual unity of the Hebrew Bible, Israel's socio-religious life, and the consistency of its meaning in the New Testament. Eichrodt (1961, 31) asserted that Christian theology has lost battle to comparative study of religions, and to re-install the studies of Hebrew Bible and Old Testament theology into Christian theology, we must succeed in approaching the Bible in a new way.

Eichrodt attempted to differentiate between thematic approach and Christian dogmatics. The study of the Hebrew Bible is not Christian dogma, rather is its predecessor. It is to defend ourselves from the stereotype Christian teachings that only make sense to the Christian community but not to the Jews. It may not be even what the original intention of the historic writings contained in the Hebrew Bible. Eichrodt (1961, 33) pleaded that the study of Old Testament theology and themes should align themselves with the teachings in the Hebrew Bible.

Thematic approach is valuable but deductive in nature. Using the theme "covenant" to interpret the passages of the Hebrew Bible may obtain arbitrary results. When focus on the theme of "covenant," it becomes a lens and everything must read through that lens. But one could have ignored other details that might possibly shared lights to the text, apart from the covenant perspective. If the Psalm 23 is read in the perspective of "covenant," then it is not the understanding of Yahweh is the shepherd in David's terms, but that Yahweh, in his covenant relationship, be to David as if a shepherd. Which covenant presents Yahweh as shepherd? Perhaps, it is a question without an answer. Reading metaphor through the theme approach is unfitting to the essence of metaphor. The study of metaphor requires the examination of a pattern or concept through various genres in the biblical literature. Preconceived idea or theme may direct our attention to its related details other than to some important yet critical information, that often may correct our understanding of the pattern or concept we are studying. This requires an inductive method of exegesis, that which is critical to the study of metaphor. Exegesis of the text must be the foundation of interpretation in explaining the meaning of the text prior to the application of critical method. The pattern or concept is derived from the biblical texts that which requires literary skills. Exegetical method is utilized to make known the meaning of the metaphor in the context of the biblical literature. Therefore, thematic approach, in Eichrodt's terms, which inclines overtly to confessional theology, is inappropriate for the study of metaphor.

Historic Progression of Revelation

The historic progression of revelation approach is exemplified by Geerhardus Vos (1975). This approach is commonly used to do biblical theology; however, it may be appropriate for the study of metaphor. Vos (1975, 5) defined that, "Biblical Theology is that branch of Exegetical Theology which deals with the process of the self-revelation of God deposited in the Bible." It means that biblical theology is derived from careful exegesis of the biblical texts. We should perceive the written text of the Bible as an activity of God's divine interpretation progressively revealing the meaning of such an activity (Vos 1975, 5). It distinct from the thematic approach of Eichrodt (1961), in that it does not confine the unfolding of the revelation of God to a single theme, rather it depends on the exegesis of the revealing activity in the course of history.

There are four features in this historic progression of revelation approach, according to Vos (1975, 5–16). First, it is "the historic progressiveness of the revelation." It is a process, rather than finality. Second, "the actual embodiment of revelation in history." Third, it is "the organic nature of the historic process observable in revelation." Fourth, it is "in its features stipulated the focus of doing biblical theology is the progression of history that which reveals the revelation." The ultimate direction of this approach leads toward "a History of Doctrine for Biblical times" rather than an exegetical approach (Vos 1975, 13).

The historic progression of revelation approach has contributed invaluably to biblical scholarship, but it inclines more toward history than literature. The concentration is on the unfolding of revelation in history. However, the study of metaphor requires high literary skills, than skills to analyze historical events. Vos (1975) believed that the revelation of God hidden is revealed through historical events and is progressive. In other words, it does not paint the ultimate picture immediately, but will show a fraction of the picture each time a historical event unfolded. Yet, this takes literary skills to analyze the literary structure and style in order to unfold the meaning of the literary piece. Besides, the Bible is undeniably a literary masterpiece. Literary skill is necessary in exegesis and interpretation of the literary text in order to understand a metaphor in its preliminary and developed form.

To unfold the metaphor that is in literary form, we must study it as literature, with the history of Israel as the background information for careful exegesis of the Hebrew Bible. The historic progression of revelation approach leans too heavily on historical unfolding and neglect the literary wrapping that must be unwrapped. Reading metaphor must focus on the historical–literary nature of the Bible and exegesis must be done in the historical–literary conventions of genres (see Barton 1996, 8–19). Therefore, the historic progression of revelation approach according to Vos, which is historical approach that lacks emphasis on literary approaches, is inappropriate for the study of metaphor.

Canonical Approach

The canonical approach is championed by the Yale scholar, Brevard S. Childs (1985). In rebutting the tyranny of historicism of his time, Childs proposed a canonical approach in biblical studies, with the intention to correct the distortion of the Bible generated from the historical–critical approach. The purpose of the approach is not only to avoid the pitfalls of historical approach, but also to discover the theological aspects of biblical literature (Childs 1985, 1).

This approach differs from other approaches in the conviction of the received texts on the "received traditions of Israel" (Childs 1985, 6).The scripture is received as the canon of the Christian faith, and the interpretation should be aligned within the canonical understanding of the scriptural texts. Childs's objective is to determine theologies from the text, and let the text speaks for itself. However, the text, according to Childs (1985, 6), cannot be isolated from the other texts of the Bible containing similar contents.

Childs advocated that hermeneutics concerns one's perception of history. Theological meaning becomes the access point render to believers (Childs 1985, 6). Childs (1985, 9) added that the task of biblical theology is the exploration of the Hebrew Bible and New Testament, and the Old Testament theology is performing the similar task only in one part of that canon as Christian scripture. The way to do Old Testament theology or the study of metaphor, in this approach, is bound by the limits of the canon. It may be said as prescriptive theological reflection, rather than descriptive reflection. Traditions as perceived in the canon, that is the Bible, position as a guide to interpretation (Childs 1985, 12). However, Childs is not lucid in his meaning of canon, of which I presumed he meant the entire Bible.

The canonical approach, advocated by Childs (1970), is a not method, rather a context for biblical interpretation. It is not so much a technique, but a perspective. This perspective shapes the way one interprets the biblical texts, in every aspect. It functions as a framework for interpretation. But reading the Bible through a lens of certain framework could be subjective and arbitrary. The strength of Childs's proposition is the treatment of the biblical text as the final product of literary work, and work on the finished product. The pre–critical text is no longer essential to the exegesis and interpretation. Scholars have been pursuing the original text to determine the meaning of the biblical literature, but there are too many uncertainties regarding the accuracy of those manuscripts. To Childs, the Bible is the inspired word of God, and the finalized form is in our possessions. This is the canonical text that governs the faith and practices of the Christian community. To Childs, the canonicity of the Bible is the presupposition of the canonical approach, and exegesis must build upon this approach.

Metaphorical language, however, belongs to literary study, and literary skills are required. It is not simply studying the text in its final textual form; it needs to exegete the text in its literary and historical contexts, and that includes the history of the ancient Near East. Metaphorical language is a form of figurative language and that it requires understanding of the grammars, sentence structure, syntax, semantics, and the culture of that particular language. To fully understand a metaphor, the exegete must examine comparative literature in order to grasp the meaning in the larger contexts that is beyond the contexts of the Bible; extrabiblical and other related literature may form part of the sources of the research.

The canonical approach is confessional in nature. Childs (1979, 71, 83) attempted to defend it as descriptive, but he contradicted himself in his explanation of the approach. Do not misunderstand that confessional approach is negative. It has its positive effects especially relating to church or Christian practices. But limiting biblical studies to Christian traditions may shape our biblical knowledge to be a lop-sided theological concept. Christian traditions should be the result of biblical studies, not the reverse. The study of metaphor requires exegetical and literary skills to understand the pattern or concept in the biblical contexts, that which involve social, economic, political, and historical.

The flaw of canonical approach is in the ambiguity of Childs's writings. In the defense of canonical books, and to refute the deficiency of historical criticism, Childs failed to elucidate the canonical approach in candid writings. It is difficult to understand what he meant by canon, and within canonical traditions, without qualifying what constituted as canon. At times, the impressions infer the Bible as canon, but at times, incline to canon–within–canon ideology.

The canonical approach stems from the presupposition that historical method fails to do justice to the Christian scripture. There are three points regarding the criticism of Childs (1979, 40–41) to historical method. First, the emergence and exercise of historical criticism fails to explain the "canonical literature" with the faith community in mind, but concerns itself in the formation of the "Hebrew literature" and also its pre-critical text and post-critical text stages. Second, the historical–critical interest overshadows the religious consciousness in the Hebrew literature. This religious consciousness, Childs believed, is invaluable information pertaining to the formation of the literary scope, shape, and structure in its inter-textual relationships. Third, the historical criticism destroys the religious impression once the faith community embraced, to this literature. Just as Childs concluded that the nature of canon poses problem to its authority to the faith community and their practices, and the way they shape and preserve it. With the introducing of historical criticism, the sacredness of the canon within the community of faith has been marred. Canonical criticism, according to Childs, is a perspective aims to recover this lack of religiosity of the faith community.

This understanding of canon in relation to the Hebrew Bible is not convincing and worst, confusing. Practices of Christian faith should have a basis of unchanging truth that is known as authority to the faith community. This authority is found in the Hebrew Bible. To say that the Hebrew Bible is authoritative to the faith community of Christians, in Childs's term, is bizarre to any reasonable mind. Practices of faith that based on canonical books should conform to the teachings stipulated in the canon. One must believe that the canonical books are the truth of all truths, or in Christian doctrine, infallible. But if the teachings of the canonical traditions are the product of the studies of the Hebrew Bible, and in return guards the interpretation of the Hebrew Bible, which is its basis, it is ironical and contradictory. The Hebrew Bible should be the basis of the canonical traditions, and this relationship must not be reversed. Therefore, the canonical approach in the format according to Childs is inappropriate for the study of metaphor.

The Hebrew Bible plays a critical role in the formation of Christian canon. I mentioned Christian canon as opposed to the understanding of the Jewish community, in that they perceived only the Hebrew Bible as canon. However, the Hebrew Bible as part of the Christian canon should shape the formation of the practices in the community of the Christian faith. The canonicity of Christian faith in return obeyed its teachings, and learned from the interpretations given to it. The question should be raised by the practitioners of the Christian faith on the handling of changing doctrines due to new or revised interpretations arose from the academic or scholarly community. I must admit that this is a hard question, and there is no easy answer. It may also raise another related question; which interpretation is correct and how does one determine it.

It is important for us to understand that our knowledge of the Hebrew Bible is not exhaustive to fully understand the language in the holy writ. In exegesis, there is a linguistic aspect, and a literary aspect. Linguistically, the Hebrew used in the writings of the Hebrew Bible, commonly known as Biblical Hebrew, resembles the classical Hebrew, which is different from the Modern Hebrew. We must first understand the Biblical Hebrew in its ancient literary meaning, before we can interpret it. Literary, the Hebrew Bible contains literary works of ancient writings that are too distant from our contemporary world. We must understand the literature in its ancient world and culture prior to interpreting it. Exegetes have to labor diligently to discover the plausible meaning or conjectural meanings of the biblical texts. At some instances, only conjectural meaning can be ascertained.

Biblical research should dig deep to find the original meaning which may be unknown to the modern minds. Questions to which is the correct interpretation, the answer is that there is none. It is not about which is correct or incorrect, rather which is appropriate or inappropriate interpretation. The canonical text is the only source for exegesis and interpretation that we can have to contribute to the community of Christian faith and practices. Therefore, the exegetical and interpretive works of biblical scholars should shape the canonical traditions, and must exercise discretion in determining the appropriate interpretations of the canonical texts, such as the Hebrew Bible. The development of the canonical approach did not end with the work of Childs, but further developed by John Sailhamer, who elucidated the concept better than his predecessor.

Sailhamer (1995) developed the canonical approach to be formulate a ca nonical theology to the Old Testament, or the Hebrew Bible. He defined, "Old Testament theology is the study and presentation of what is revealed in the Old Testament" (Sailhamer 1995, 17). To achieve this end, one must fully embrace the canonical approach, and that means accept and work on the texts as in its final form. It is from the text that we derive theology, and Old Testament theology must adopt a textual approach, rather than examine independent events (Sailhamer 1995, 199). Sailhamer (1995, 222) believed that the text of the Hebrew Bible should be the basis of theological interpretation, rather than a text that reconstructed from the pre-critical text. Distinct to the historic progression of revelation approach which dependent on unfolding historical events, Sailhamer focused on textual studies of the biblical literature. In this perspective, Old Testament theology in the canonical context is "confessional," not "descriptive" (Sailhamer 1995, 224). Sailhamer (1995, 224) stated, "The recognition of the OT as the Word of God entails treating it as a special book." On this token, Sailhamer approached the Old Testament theology diachronically with what the texts reveal. The canonical approach is exhibited explicitly in Sailhamer's (1995, 237) words, "The historical dynamics of the formation of the Hebrew Bible, we believe, are such that a diachronic approach to its theology is the most appropriate methods."

What is obvious about this canonical criticism is that exegesis must base on the final form of the biblical text. Sailhamer advocated this point. The pre-critical text, though fascinates the research process, it does not necessary add insights to the text. Besides, tracing the literary development of the Hebrew Bible is difficult and tedious. As time advances, distance between two cultural worlds is farther. The best and reliable ancient text of the Hebrew Bible is the Masoretic Text. It is the only possible source to understand the events pertaining to the Israelite nation and Yahweh. Our attention should focus on this preserved and received text, and should no longer meddle with the pre-critical text development.

The concern we should have towards the historical development of the Hebrew Bible is the area of comparative literature. Not that the Hebrew Bible is inferior to those other ancient texts, but one should understand concepts and literary forms used in its contemporary literary works, especially those from the ancient Near Eastern. There are many historical information not recorded in the biblical literature, one may be frustrated with the lack of resources to attain plausible understanding of the biblical text. Biblical history, after all, is selective history. Many events happened alongside the mainstream history that is obscured to the common knowledge. Comparing related literature will enlarge our historical horizon and that often help one in the understanding of the biblical event. Literary skills are essential in reading the biblical text because the Bible is literature. Sailhamer (1995, 87-88) rightly coined a term "literature-criticism" to describe an approach broader than literary criticism. It includes the various critical methods in the studies of the Hebrew Bible such as literary, source, form, tradition, and structural (Sailhamer 1995, 88). This term describes correctly the perspective we must have in doing exegesis.

I defer from Sailhamer in that doing theological concepts of the Old Testament is descriptive rather than confessional. Confessional is a synonym of prescriptive, and is no difference from doing systematic theology. Theology is prescriptive in approach and abstract. But theological themes such a shepherd metaphor defers from systematic theology in that the concepts derived from the biblical text are not abstract. It is relational because it relates to the development of one's faith, or one's relationship with God. Besides, it is not arrange under major headings in a systematic manner. It flows from the text to the reader, and that the theological meaning of the metaphor explicitly displays itself to the exegete, in its original context. Confessional approach will confine the study of the Hebrew Bible to a prescriptive framework that dictates what should and should not do in exegesis. The study of metaphor is descriptive, not prescriptive. Metaphorical figures are expressed through the literary skills of language. The moment we approach a concept in a confessional manner, we examine it with a preconceived idea. The results of exegesis may be swayed by personal bias towards confessional faith or traditions. We must understand that canonical traditions must reflect the contributions of scholarship, which is the source for restructuring and formulation of our Christian traditions, not the reverse. Therefore, the canonical approach exhibited by Sailhamer is inappropriate to the study of metaphor.

Christ-Events or Redemptive-Historical Approach

This approach is called the "Christ-events" or redemptive historical, which is also often used to do biblical theology. Graeme L. Goldsworthy (1991) is a proponent of this approach. He defines,

> Biblical theology is concerned with God's saving acts and his word as these occur within the history of the people of God. It follows the progress of revelation from the first word of God to man through to the unveiling of the full glory of Christ." (Goldsworthy 1991, 37)

The center of this approach is Christ. Goldsworthy advocated that we must read the Bible with Christ and the related events as a pattern for exegesis. This approach ushers every passage into the mould of "Christ-events" and interpret through that pattern. It is a valuable approach to relate the Hebrew Bible and New Testament. However, it reads the Hebrew Bible from the perspective of the New Testament.

According to Goldsworthy (1991, 38), biblical theology should be included in the exegetical theology. Exegesis is explaining what the text mean, and thus theology derives. Goldsworthy (1991, 38) stated that textual criticism is one of the steps in doing biblical theology, and its objective is to recover the original text through comparing with other available ancient texts in its language, and the investigation of the history of these texts. At best, textual criticism recovers the most reliable text. Apart from textual criticism, Goldsworthy (1991, 39) included literary and source criticism, tradition history, form criticism and redaction criticism.

According to Goldsworthy (1991, 40), biblical theology, with "Christ-events," concerns grammatical and literary conventions, which is also known as historical-grammatical method. Distinct to historical-critical method, it requires the analysis of grammar in its historical context. The pre-critical text is no longer a concern, but the final form of the biblical texts (Goldsworthy 1991, 41). The difference between Childs (1985, 1979) and Goldsworthy (1991) is that the former proposes a perspective toward biblical study, and the latter formulates a center for the study of biblical theology. Although Goldsworthy embraced a canonical perspective of the Bible, he prioritized to formulate "Christ-events" as a center to do biblical theology. As for Childs, he is concerned about the framework that shapes the study of the biblical literature as canon.

The question may need to ask is, "what is exegesis?" In non–technical terms, exegesis is the forerunner of biblical theology, and the result of exegesis forms the theological concepts that are in the biblical contexts (Goldsworthy 1991, 41). Reading the Hebrew Bible in light of the significance of Christ's life and work, it ties together every passage in the canon to that center that explicates its meaning, including those that are controversial. This happens because Christ is God's manifestation in human form on earth, and an icon of his presence (Col 1:15). Goldsworthy (1991, 97) stated that, "It brings to full clarity what has been present in the Old Testament as a shadow from the beginning." Therefore, it is important that biblical theology deals with the events in light of Christ's life and work, not on the philosophical speculation of ideas or concepts, so that appropriate interpretation can be determined in the biblical literature (Goldsworthy 1991, 98). Particularly in the studies of the Hebrew Bible, biblical theology strengthens its relationship with the New Testament. It also strengthens the unity of the Bible. Interpretation of biblical texts must juxtapose the texts in its proper context. Someone well said that, "A text without a context is a pre-text" (cited by Goldsworthy 1981, 28). Goldsworthy understands that the Bible is not an anthology with religious meaning. Rather, it is given by divine intention. It has coherence relationship in within. The traditional treatise is to distinct Hebrew Bible from New Testament, and the result is the emergence of Old Testament theology and New Testament theology. But if biblical theology deals with the materials of the entire Bible, Hebrew Bible and New Testament, then the inter-textual relationship is essential to preserve its unity. The events in the Bible are records of various eras, and understand their relationships will enlighten our understanding of God's revealed words (Goldsworthy 1981, 40).

Doing biblical theology requires adoption of presuppositions regarding the Bible, according to Goldsworthy (1981, 30). First, we must acknowledge that the Bible is literature. Second, it has human history as its background, it run along with this historical timeline and forms part of historical events. Third, it has a "theological dimension" exhibit in history that which is God's intervention in human history, God and the world. Goldsworthy (1981, 40) stated that the history of the Bible is "a theological history." These exhibitions of God's acts are recorded in literary form. Due to the nature of the written word of God, we must, according to Goldsworthy (1981, 40), flow with the movement of the events to understand its meaning.

There is similarity between the approaches of Vos (1975) and Goldsworthy (1981, 1991) toward biblical theology. Like Vos, Goldsworthy approached the Bible with the perspective that revelation is progressive through history. Unlike Vos, Goldsworthy (1981, 41) hinged the approach on "God's redeeming activity to man" in Christ's life and work. Goldsworthy (1981, 41–42) further explicated the history of redemption. First, it is "progressive." The readers should pay attention to the climaxes in the biblical events. Second, it is "incomplete without the New Testament." In other words, the Hebrew Bible is explained by the New Testament's understanding of Christ's life and work. Third, it is "to be interpreted."

This method of interpretation of the Hebrew Bible has three implications. First, we must examine the Hebrew Bible from the New Testament because in Christ, we are made the children of God (Jn 1:12). Second, the Hebrew Bible is the foundation of the New Testament. Third, the Hebrew Bible directs the progression of historical events to a common goal and that "which is fulfilled in Christ" (Goldsworthy 1981, 42).

The approach of Goldsworthy is seemingly appropriate and sound to do biblical theology, but inappropriate for the study of metaphor. It seems logical to examine the Hebrew Bible in the understanding of the New Testament. However, this approach appears to be deductive than inductive. It is not about which is correct or incorrect approach. Rather, it is about which method of biblical study is best to achieve the objective of balanced perspective in exegesis and interpretation. The approach of "Christ-events" may read the theological ideas of New Testament into the passages of the Hebrew Bible, even these ideas may not be found there. Using the life and work of Christ as a center of interpretation may fall into the pitfalls of thematic approach; that is, missing other information that may shed insights to the text. The pattern of "Christ-events" is incomprehensive to deal with the entire Bible. Redemptive history as the foreground in the "Christ-events" approach cannot explain redemptive purpose beginning in Genesis chapters 1 and 2, except through theological deduction. The most dialectical correlation of the Hebrew Bible and New Testament can only be traced to Genesis chapter 3, that is where the promise of redemption given in verse 15 after the Fall. But before that, it is a weak argument to support the existence of redemptive history utilizing "Christ-events" approach (Goldsworthy 1981).

The study of metaphor requires literary skills in exegesis combine with historical knowledge. Redemptive historical approach crippled itself by enclosing with Christ's life and work. Conjectural meaning may be derived by injecting those interpreted "Christ-events" into our readings of the Hebrew Bible. Metaphor, however, requires exegesis of the linguistic skills expressed through the texts, and not by reading concepts from interpreted events into the biblical texts. The concept of the metaphor must be discovered through the literary progression of the written words, and allowed the text lead the way to understanding. Thus, the "Christ–events" or redemptive historical approach is inappropriate for the study of metaphor.

Historical-Literary Approach

This approach is based on the presupposition that the Bible is literature embraced within the spectrum of history. Therefore, it requires literary skills that apply to the relevant historical contexts. The choice of the term "literary" rather than "grammatical" is deliberate. The former expresses a broader range of literary skills, while the latter limits to language. The historical–literary approach focuses on the literary-analytical investigation and the historical approach to criticism. Exegesis must be based on the Hebrew text and the meaning is derived from the text. This exegetical approach presupposes that the biblical literature is unfolded in the progression of history. Through historical events and writings, the meaning of the biblical literature is revealed.

There are three major areas in doing exegesis. They are not in sequential importance. First, it is the historical context. This area does not limit to historical timeline. It should also include social, political, economic, and religious dimensions relating to the text. Second, it is the literary context. To do this requires the application of source criticism, literary criticism, tradition criticism, redaction criticism, and rhetorical criticism. Third, it is the philological context. It concerns about grammars, syntax, semantics, and semiotics. Other linguistics theory may be utilized when necessary to determine meaning from peculiar genre.

The difference between historical–critical and historical–literary method is the presupposition in exegesis. Traditionally, the historical–critical method was employed to ascertain the historical veracity of the Bible through questioning beyond the literary limits of the finalized biblical text. Thus, it was abused by the liberals to falsify the authenticity of the Bible, and the result affected its religiosity. The historical–literary method aims to return the religiosity to the Bible through embracing the finalized biblical text as the starting point and investigate through the means of historical criticism and literary analysis. Recognizing that the Bible has a religious nature is critical to the exegetical meaning. The historical–literary exegesis places the Bible at the center of research and counter check with all possible scholarly and academic works, so that the meaning is revealed and at the same time, ascertained the veracity of the biblical text.

The historical literary exegesis fulfils the requirements to study metaphor.

Literary skills will explain the meaning contains in the language, and the historical knowledge juxtaposes the meaning in light of its historical setting. In so doing, the metaphor is derived from exegesis, not theological deduction, and is understood in the contexts of its historical implication.

In summary, the historical literary approach is a method for the study of metaphor. The following chapters will embrace this approach with the objective to obtain a balanced perspective of the metaphor of shepherd. Now, let us observe the image of shepherd in the Hebrew Bible.

CHAPTER THREE

THE IMAGE OF SHEPHERD
IN THE HEBREW BIBLE

The image of shepherd existed long ago in the Hebrew Bible; it was not exclusively New Testament image. Traditionally, pastoral image in the church was closely kneaded to the New Testament teachings of shepherd, and rarely referred to the Hebrew Bible. In this chapter, we are to explore the shepherd image portrayed in the Hebrew Bible. As this chapter focuses on the idea of shepherd in the Hebrew Bible, references to the ancient Near Eastern literature will be brief.

Comparison of the Shepherd Metaphor
in the Literature of the Hebrew Bible
and the Ancient Near Eastern

The literature of the ancient Near Eastern and the Hebrew Bible provide the various shades of the metaphorical figure such as leading, feeding, and protecting. They provide a proportionate sense of these shades of the metaphor. The shepherd figure is prominent in Psalm 23 as a metaphor used on Yahweh. It forms one of the bases of New Testament shepherding theology. Yahweh is the divine shepherd and it is in two-folds, shepherd-king and shepherd-god.

The king is considered a shepherd or a leader in the ancient Near Eastern literature. He is believed to have authority given by deity. The myth of Etana regards kingship in this way,

> Scepter, crown, tiara, and (shepherd's) crook
> Lay deposited before Anu in heaven,
> There being no counseling for its people.
> (Then) kingship descended from heaven. (Pritchard 1969, 114A–1i).[1]

Similarly, the literature of the Hebrew Bible treats Yahweh as shepherd and king of Israel from the emergence of Israel nation. A biblical character of the patriarchal period manifests the quality of a shepherd. Yahweh made a covenant with Abraham in Genesis 12:1–3, and through him, his entire household, born or bought, will be blessed, because Yahweh's covenant shall remain in his descendants "an everlasting covenant" (Ge 17:13 NIV). The imputed authority vested upon Abraham made him a channel of blessings to his people in his household.

The Hebrew Bible also considers god as a shepherd. Yahweh ushers the Israelites his people through the wilderness "like a flock by the hand of Moses and Aaron" (Ps 77:20 NIV). He, as the divine shepherd, passes on the shepherding responsibility of his people to his earthly shepherd such as David (2 Sa 5:2; 7:7–8). Thus, David a king is also connoted as shepherd-king. A dual shepherd figure is embedded in Davidic rule. Yahweh divinely delivers the Israelites to the promised land will also ensure that a worthy shepherd shall shepherd them because the unworthy shepherd scattered his flock (Jer 23:1) and fed on them (Eze 34:7–10). The dual shepherd figure of Davidic shepherding signifies the twofold aspects of the shepherd metaphor as shepherd-king and shepherd-god in the literature of the Hebrew Bible, somewhat similar in the ancient Near Eastern literature. To further explore the metaphor of shepherd, we shall now turn to the study of shepherd-king metaphor in the Hebrew Bible.

The Shepherd-King Metaphor in the Hebrew Bible

As mentioned earlier, the early leaders of the Israelites prior to the monarchy are described by Yahweh as shepherds (2 Sa 7:7, see 1 Ch 17:6; however, a context of "leading" may be possible in that Yahweh describes his relationship with Israel as a "walk", hālak) (Brettler 1989, 36–37).[2] The rulers that come after are listed as priests, shepherds and prophets (Jer 2:8). According to Marc Zvi Brettler (1989, 36), the designation of shepherd to kings is one of the oldest titles among many in the ancient Near East.

The shepherding function most often used with the shepherd-king figure is that of leading.[3] For example, Joshua is the shepherd "to go out" before the people and "come in before them," "lead them out and bring them in" (Nu 27:17 NIV).

The second shepherding function connected to the shepherd-king metaphor is that of feeding. Yahweh has promised that a day when there will be shepherd who will lead the flock with "knowledge and understanding" (Jer 3:15 NIV).[4] Notice that the word "lead" can be translated as "feed" in the Hebrew word "raʿah." In other words, the shepherd–king should lead by feeding them with necessary knowledge and directive to life, especially their religious life. Historically and prophetically, David became king of Israel and Israel was prosperous. He ruled with power of Yahweh, and the surrounding nations feared the Israel nation because of Yahweh. Prophetically, Yahweh will set David over Israel his flock and "will tend them" (Eze 34:23 NIV). This also implies another way of tending by feeding.

The third activity of shepherd-king is to provide protection to the afflicted sheep, the people. The flock is vulnerable when there is no shepherd, or when the shepherd lacks understanding (Zec 10:2–3; Isa 56:11). A foolish shepherd will abandon the flock and leave to the mercy of the devourer. The lost sheep will be broken and scattered (Zec 11:16–17). Therefore, the shepherd is to shield the sheep from harm.

The provision of protection also has a function of keeping the flock from scattering. For example, the unrighteous shepherds in Jeremiah 10:21 (NIV) illustrates that the actions without divine guidance from Yahweh will scatter the flocks, "The shepherds are senseless and do not inquire of the LORD; so they do not prosper and all their flock is scattered."

The three activities of shepherd-king; leading, feeding, and protecting, must depend on two foundations. The first is tender care. This is an application of the shepherd metaphor display in love and care for the flock. Ezekiel 34:4 and Zechariah 11:16 depict the picture of the unrighteous shepherds. They did not care for Yahweh's flock; they did not strengthen the diseased, heal the sick or bind the broken. A righteous shepherd will be one who seeks out the straying from the flock (Eze 34:4–6, 8; Zec 11:16).[5] Thus, a shepherd-king is like the righteous shepherd who does likewise; tend the flock with love and care.

The second is faithfulness to responsibilities. For example, Cyrus, who was regarded as Yahweh's shepherd, used this nuances. He was referred as one who would perform the work of Yahweh (Isa 44:28), portrayed his faithfulness to the task assigned.

Of the three activities defined within the metaphor of shepherd-king figure in the Hebrew Bible, leading is a prominent shepherding activity. Feeding and protecting are in decreasing frequency. The figure of shepherd-king presupposes that righteousness brings deliverance from distress. This foundational presupposition is evident in the Hebrew Bible. Without a righteous shepherd there is no strength (1 Ki 22:17, see 2 Ch 18:16). Likewise, without a righteous king there is no power in the nation (Dt 17:18–20).

The category used for the shepherd-king figure has vividly expressed the essentials of deliverance. The feeding aspect of the shepherding activity is a figure for deliverance, not necessarily the eating of physical food. Unfaithful shepherds do not feed the flock but the flock, "has become food for all the wild animals, and because my shepherds did not search for my flock but cared for themselves rather than my flock" (Eze 34:8 NIV). Restoration from trouble like this fits the favorite description of the feeding of sheep metaphor (Jer 3:15; Eze 34:23). In light of comparing the close connection between the shepherd-king and the shepherd-god concepts discussed earlier, one may discover similar "deliverance from distress" theme in the study of shepherd–God metaphor in the literature of the Hebrew Bible, as well as ancient Near Eastern literature.[6]

The Shepherd-God Metaphor in the Hebrew Bible

Territorial concept of deity is prominent in the ancient world. The god worshiped in a region is regarded as shepherd over the people; any human authority is a shepherd vested with authority from the divine shepherd, the gods. In comparison, the ancient Near Eastern literature rarely uses the figure of shepherd-god as an epithet, but the figure of shepherd-king. On the other hand, the Hebrew Bible employs the figure of shepherd-god as the one who leads his people (ssm, "lead, guide, show", see Schafer 1905, 91, line 14; 93, line 16; Gardiner 1957, 592; Pritchard 1969, 448a–b).[7]

The usage of the shepherd-god metaphor in the ancient Near Eastern literature and the literature of the Hebrew Bible mostly related to distress or deliverance activity. It is often regarded the god as the one who delivers the people from distress, whether described by the activities of leading, providing, or some other shepherding activities. This figure has references in the Hebrew Bible, explicitly and implicitly, as well.

Explicit references to the shepherd-god figure designate Yahweh as a shepherd (rō'eh) or in which Yahweh is the subject of the verb rā'āh. However, the shepherd-god figure is also implicit in those references in which the people are designated as sheep.

Yahweh as the shepherd is explicitly stated in references employing the verb rā'āh. By its lexical definition, the verb means "pasture, tend, graze, keep" (Holladay 1971, s. v. rā'āh). The outstanding example of this is Jonah 3:7 where (rā'āh) is placed with šātāh (drink) and both are aspects of ṭā'am (taste) in the exhortation of the king that no man or beast is to taste anything; they may not eat or drink. Of almost 60 uses of rā'āh in non-figurative contexts, only 16 have to do with feeding of sheep.[8] The participial form rō'eh in non-figurative contexts is usually a frozen nomen agentis simply for "shepherd."

One of the most extensively used of the shepherd-god metaphor in the Hebrew Bible is in Ezekiel 34. The verb rā'āh is used of Yahweh five times; "I will pasture," "I will tend," "I myself will tend," and "I will shepherd" (Eze 34:13, 14, 15, 16 NIV). Implicit shepherding indicators are also present mare'it (pasturage), nāweh (abode), and ṣō'n (sheep). The employment of shepherding words in this chapter reveals that this is a major theme and presents the most extensive inventory of divine shepherding activities in the Hebrew Bible.

There are many contexts where the shepherd-god figure is used explicitly of Yahweh; it is, however, difficult to assign a single precise qualifying shepherding activity to rāʿāh. For example, in Genesis 48:15–16 (NIV), the verb rāʿāh is placed between "God before whom my fathers . . . walked" and "Angel who has delivered me." It refers to Yahweh's safe leading of Jacob through the situations of his life, especially in the leaving and returning to the land of Canaan. This is an explicit reference to Yahweh as shepherd but in the recollection of historical event. Perhaps at the point of the incident, it was not obvious that Yahweh was shepherding. It is the reflection of Jacob that realizing Yahweh was leading him through his life journey, though he may not have fully apprehended the shepherding activity of Yahweh. It is through his words that expressed his understanding of who Yahweh is to him.

The second explicit passage with leading as the shepherding activity is Isaiah 40:11. Yahweh tells the messenger to cry out to the captives in Babylon that he will surely come to take up the rulership of his people (Isa 40:10). He will "tend" (rāʿāh) his flock (ʿēder), "gathers the lambs" (yĕqabbēṣ) in his arms, "carries them" (iśśāʾ) and "leads those" (yĕnahēl) (Isa 40:11 NIV).

Yahweh, the one who scattered Israel will "gather" (qābaṣ) and "watch" (šāmar) him as a "shepherd" (rōʿeh) over his "flock" (ʿēder) (Jer 31:10 NIV). The text continues with a description of the ransoming and redeeming of Jacob and the return of the people to Zion (Jer 31:11–12). Though leading may be the specific shepherding activity, its overriding significance is as a figure of speech to describe the deliverance of distress out of captivity. For example, the verb nāśāʾ (lift) is used in the shepherding context of Isaiah 40:11 of the captive weary sheep on the drive. This carrying activity is, however, within the call for salvation in a lament.

The designation of shepherd of Israel (rōʿeh yiśrāʿēl) is placed in parallelism to "you who lead Joseph like a flock" (nōhēg kaṣʾōn yôsēp) (Ps 80:1 NIV). When in need of salvation, the community implored the divine shepherd to lead them out of distress. This request appears in a larger context of Micah 7:14–20 (NIV),

> Shepherd your people with your staff, the flock of your inheritance, which lives by itself in a forest, in fertile pasturelands. Let them feed in Bashan and Gilead as in days long ago. "As in the days when you came out of Egypt, I will show them my wonders." Nations will see and be ashamed, deprived of all their power. They will lay their hands on their mouths and their ears will become deaf. They will lick dust like a snake, like creatures that crawl on the ground. They will come trembling out of their dens; they will turn in fear to the LORD our God and will be afraid of you. Who is a God like you, who pardons sin and forgives the transgression of the remnant of his inheritance? You do not stay angry forever but delight to show mercy. You will again have compassion on us; you will tread our sins underfoot and hurl all our iniquities into the depths

of the sea. You will be true to Jacob, and show mercy to Abraham, as you pledged on oath to our fathers in days long ago.

In this passage, we see that the prophet expressed a prayer for Yahweh to act (7:14) and a confident statement that Yahweh will return to his people and defeat Israel's enemies (7:15–20). Although the shepherding activity of Yahweh in Micah 7:14–20 is a saving activity that directs to the forthcoming captivity, it addresses Yahweh as the shepherd. He is the one who will deliver the people of Israel, just as he had delivered them from Egypt in a marvelous manner.

The final explicit shepherding reference to Yahweh involves the deliverance of the sheep from distress. The scenario is used of a place of safety where a man is able to see any danger coming, and as such is a metaphor for salvation (2 Sa 22:20; Ps 18:20; 31:9; 118:5). This describes a dangerous place where the sheep has no quick protection (cf. Keil and Delitzsch 1986, 10:83). Yahweh as the shepherd will lead his sheep, David, to the pasture that is free and safe.

In summary, when Yahweh is explicitly called a shepherd, the shepherding activity describes in the eight contexts is delivering out of distress. But we must observe further the implicit references of the shepherd–god metaphor.

The foremost shepherding activity emerging from the implicit references to Yahweh as the shepherd is also that of leading. This leading is specifically applied to two events in the history of Israelite nation—the exodus out of Egypt and the restoration of Israel from the captivity of Babylon. Moses, in his song celebrating the overthrown of the Egyptian army, describes how Yahweh "lead" (nāhāh) his redeemed people, "guide" them (nāhal) to his "holy dwelling" ("habitation", nāweh; Ex 15:13 NIV).[9]

Leading activity of shepherding is also expressed in terms of restoration. Jeremiah described how the wicked shepherds had scattered the sheep (ṣō'n) of Yahweh's pasture (mir'eh) (23:1 NIV). They "have scattered" them but Yahweh "will gather" ('ŏqabbēṣ) his flock (ṣō'n) and "bring them" (šób) again to "their pasture" (nāweh) (Jer 23:2–3; 50:19 NIV).

This leading activity of the shepherd in the context of restoration is closely related to the gathering of a flock of sheep already in the land. Micah saw the restoration as a time when Yahweh will "gather" ('āsap) all of Jacob, "bring" (qābaṣ) the remnant of Israel, and "bring them together" (yahad 'ăśîmennû, lit. "set them together") as "sheep" (ṣō'n) in a "pen" (bāṣrāh, lit. "fence"), just as a "flock" ('ēder) in their "pasture" (dōber) (Mic 2:12 NIV).

The belief that the flock of Israel is protected from harm derived from the conviction that Israel is in a close and intimate relationship with their shepherd, Yahweh (Ps 74:1–2, 20). Yahweh is Israel's Maker and God; they are the people of his pasture (mir'eh) and the flock (ṣō'n) of his hand. This relationship depicts a picture of creator and creation, master and servants, and shepherd and sheep. It describes the bond between Yahweh and Israel right from the beginning of its history.

In Zephaniah 2:6–7, feeding and giving rest to the sheep are the two main shepherding activities. Yahweh assigns the pastures of shepherd and flocks. However, the remnant of Judah will also "will find pasture" (rāʿāh) and "lie down" (rābaṣ) in the region (Zep 2:7 NIV). Compared with the leading and gathering activities above, this passage is describing the return of the people from captivity to restoration. The point of this hypocatastasis is that the worshiper will get strength from the faithfulness of Yahweh as one gets strength from eating.

The saving activity of the sheep from distress is another activity in the implicit references to the shepherd-god figure.[10] For example, Zechariah 9:16 (NIV) shows Yahweh is going to "save" (yāšaʿ) his people from captivity as a "flock." Psalm 79 (NIV) shows a less specific distress but certainly calamity comes upon the nation of Israel. The psalmist lamented that the nations are overrunning the land, laying waste the "habitation" (nāweh) of Yahweh. They pleaded that Yahweh will reward those who are destined to die what they deserved, so that they may be vindicated. Another example would be Ezekiel 34 that uses the most extensive description of Yahweh as the shepherd, employed the metaphor to describe his saving activity to his people.

Another implicit shepherding activity of Yahweh is ensuring fertility. In describing the restoration, Ezekiel 37:26 says that Yahweh will cause the population of the land to increase like a flock (ṣōʾn).

One final implicit reference of the shepherding activity is the giving of protection. Psalm 107:41 (NIV) shows Yahweh's making the psalmist's families like "flocks" (ṣōʾn) is parallel to his setting "the needy" in a place inaccessible to any affliction. The picture is not simply deliverance from distress, though it is the key notion, it is also the blessings that come along the deliverance from Yahweh. Thus, the protection Yahweh provided comes with the blessings from his mighty power, and that the provision of protection encompasses provision of prosperity.

The implicit divine shepherd passages discussed above have an overriding aspect that is the activity of placing the flock into distress and bringing them out again. The four passages, Jeremiah 13:17, 25:30, Psalms 44:12, and 74:1, Yahweh is said to bring distress upon the people of Israel. Six passages, Exodus 15:13, Isaiah 63:11-14, Psalm 78:52, Jeremiah 23:1-3, 50:19, and Zechariah 10:3-10 employed leading activities and one passage, Micah 2:12 employed gathering activity, are used specifically of either the exodus experience or the future restoration. The two passages, Psalm 95:7-8 and 100:1-4 employed implicitly the shepherd figure, also known as *todah* psalms, are celebrating Yahweh's deliverance of Israel like shepherd over the sheep. Some of these references are related to the exodus experience or future restoration. In Zephaniah 2:7, the feeding activity is descriptive to the restoration of the remnant of Israel, that they restore the land where they find pasture, restore the rest they need from the nations, and restore their wealth that they had lost. In Zechariah 9:16 and Psalm 79:1, 7, 9, 13, Yahweh, the shepherd, is specifically said to be the one who saves. The ensuring of fertility activity in Ezekiel 36:37-38 describes the increase of population in the land after the restoration out of Babylon. This reference also points to the fact that the restoration brings glory, not just to Israel, but to Yahweh, too. One final reference used the shepherd figure to express the protection of his people is Psalm 107:41. The word "śûm" (put) indicates that Yahweh place the needy in inaccessibly high places (śāgab), in order to protect them from the perilous situation that may bring them harm. Eighteen of the nineteen references used this shepherd figure to speak either putting people under distress or delivering them from distress. In other words, when there is an implicit reference to the divine shepherd, with only one exception, distress and deliverance from the shepherd is evident.

The various contexts of the implicit shepherding references show that the flock is given over to distress. If Judah does not respond to Yahweh, Judah, Yahweh's flock ('ēder) will go into captivity (Jer 13:17). This sentiment is again expressed in Psalm 74 in elaboration.

A final consideration of the shepherd-god figure is the description of the people as sheep. This is considered an implicit reference of the shepherding activity. When the people are as designated sheep in the Hebrew Bible, it is usually an unflattering term describing the people in distress or lack of a leader. In some contexts, it describes a style of peaceful living.

When the people are described as sheep, the most common condition they are in is distress. There are three aspects of this "people as sheep in distress" metaphor. The first aspect concerning the condition of distress, as the sheep found in those passages in which similes are used to describe distress coming upon a people. For example, "The Israelites camped opposite them [Syrians] like two small flocks [ḥăśipēy] of goats ['izzim], while the Arameans covered the countryside" (1 Ki 20:27 NIV). The picture here is the desperation under the pressure of being surrounded by the enemies, and the fact that being surrounded made them felt small in the eyes of the opponents.

On the other hand, in the "people as sheep in distress" metaphor, the people are usually referred to as sheep by hypocatastasis or metaphor rather than simile. In this case, the shepherd is the one who brings the sheep into distress. For example, David, who sinfully counted the people and brought Yahweh's wrath upon Israel, inquired why God was punishing the sheep (sō'n) who had done nothing wrong (2 Sa 24:17; see 1 Ch 21:17).

Being in distress is evident when Yahweh's wrath turns against the flock. When the worshipping community fail to understand, Yahweh's anger smokes against the flock (sō'n) of his pasture (mir'eh) (Ps 74:1), distress will be the condition incurred upon them. Yahweh will roar against other flocks and pastures; he will come against the strong habitation (nāweh) of Edom and Babylon and no shepherd will stop him (Jer 49:19–20; 50:44–45). Other nations are other sources of distress upon the flock of the Israelites. Jerusalem lamented the nations have laid waste Yahweh's holy "homeland" (nāweh) (Ps 79:7 NIV). In response to distress, Yahweh's flock called to him to save them (Ps 28:9; 79:9–13; 80:2). Thus, Yahweh becomes the divine shepherd to Israel, and Israel be comes his sheep.

The divine shepherd with reference to the shepherd-god figure is the one who can also deliver from distress. This figure is applied to the nation of Israel in its two great distresses-leaving Egypt and leaving Babylon. During the exodus, Yahweh led his people to his "holy dwelling" ("habitation", nāweh; Ex 15:13 NIV). This shepherding activity during the exodus provides the basis for hoping Yahweh will deliver again his flock out of Babylon (Isa 63:10–14). The delivering of Yahweh's sheep out of captivity is a favorite figure for the restoration. Some prophets perceive the restoration as the gathering of the "flock" (ṣō'n) (Mic 2:12 NIV) when sea-coasts is "pasture" (nāweh, Zep 2:6–7 NIV) and the people will "pasture" (rō'eh) on the coasts and "lie down" (rābaṣ) without fear (Zep 3:13 NIV).

In these contexts, "the people as sheep" metaphor is used of people in distress. Either Yahweh is bringing distress upon them or the surrounding nations are troubling them. They call upon Yahweh, their shepherd, to deliver them, his needy sheep.

The second aspect of the "people as sheep" metaphor is the description of the people in need of leadership. For example, Moses implored Yahweh to set a leader over the people so that they would not be like "sheep" (ṣō'n) that "without a shepherd" (rō'eh) (Nu 27:17 NIV).

The third aspect of the "people as sheep" metaphor is the description of the peaceful state of the people who lived in Yahweh's pasture. These sheep were exhorted to feed (rā'āh) on faithfulness, "trust" Yahweh, "do good" and "dwell in the land" (Ps 37:3 NIV). Yahweh delivered the "needy" from "affliction" and placed "their families" like a "flock" (ṣō'n), that is, he protected them (Ps 107:41 NIV). Those in captivity look forward to a time of future peace. The hope of restoration is also evident in this aspect of the "people as sheep" metaphor, in that it is not only the restoration of the land or nation, but the restoration of peace that the sheep may rest in the pasture of their shepherd.

In summary, these passages employing "people as sheep" metaphor express the distress in the experiences of the people of Israel. Some are expressed in terms of needing leadership of which is the most prominent feature of the image of shepherd. Others describe the peaceful state of those who are in good relationship with Yahweh.

Summary

The shepherd-king metaphor in the Hebrew Bible embraces meanings such as that of leading, followed by feeding, seeking the lost, and protecting, is encompassed with quality of tender caring and faithfulness. Similarly, the shepherd-king metaphor in the ancient Near Eastern texts uses, in order of frequency, the figure as an epithet for ruler in, leading, protecting, providing physical needs, and bringing fertility and careful watching.

The Hebrew Bible gives a fuller inventory of shepherding activity in the figure of shepherd-god than the ancient Near Eastern materials, and in fact, equally or if not more substantial than the New Testament. The shepherd-god figure in the Hebrew Bible encompasses activity of leading and specifically leading in the ways of justice, followed by providing, guarding and watching. The overriding presupposition of these activities involves distressing situations. The divine shepherd metaphor in the context of distress is referred in many passages, explicitly and implicitly. When people are referred to as sheep, the figure expressed distress in the experiences of the people. Where the shepherd role is evident, deliverance and hope is displayed. Therefore, the divine shepherd metaphor in the Hebrew Bible is expressed in two aspects, shepherd-king and shepherd-god.

Thus far we have done is an overview of the shepherd metaphor. To have a concrete impression of this metaphor study, we must travel through the diverse genres to see how this metaphor exhibited in the major divisions of the Hebrew Bible. Now we shall turn to the metaphor of shepherd in the Torah.

Notes

1. Though the lines are fragmentary, they are parallel with "shepherd" parallel to the seeking of king: dIn-nin-ni ri-e-[a-am . . .] u sarram i-se-'-l . . .; (Langdon 1931, 9).

2. Brettler (1989) outlines in his study that the metaphor applied to God shows that "he is the ideal king" who is better than all other royal shepherd. This is true even the crook is used for "comfort," rather than punishment.

3. This is remarkably different from the non-figurative uses of the shepherd in the Hebrew Bible. Of nearly 50 uses of rāʿāh, 30 supply a nuance contextually. One half of these involve feeding (Ge 30:31; 41:2, 18; Ex 34:3; Isa 11:7; 27:10; 30:23; 65:25; Jer 6:3; Hos 9:2; Jnh 3:7, an outstanding example of this use; Job 1:14; SS 2:16; 4:5: and 1 Ch 27:29). Five times a resting in a quiet place is involved (Isa 11:7; 13:20; 27:10; SS 1:7). Watering or giving drink is seen four times (Ge 29:7; Ex 2:17, 19; and Jnh 3:7). Providing protection and shearing are each used twice (Ge 30:31; Am 3:12; and 1 Sa 25:7, 16, respectively). Healing and breeding are each used once (Isa 30:23; and Ge 30:25–43, respectively). Non-figurative uses of the shepherd do not reflect explicitly a function of leading while figurative uses of the metaphor employ leading as its most common application.

4. The kingship of Mesopotamia, symbolized by the scepter, crown/tiara and shepherd's crook, was considered as a counselor for the people in the kingdom. The feeding on knowledge and prudence in Jeremiah 3:15 is probably the counseling of the king in the proper way of Yahweh and is, therefore, another way of saying they are led by the shepherd-king into the proper way.

5. This same tender care is the job of the divinely appointed shepherd of Zechariah 11:4–14. The object lesson, Zechariah plays out for the people is to illustrate Yahweh's waning care for his people in the light of their sin. They are sheep ready for the slaughter (Zec 11:4, 7). Zechariah's actions demonstrate that Yahweh will not care for them and will let them be destroyed (Zec 11:9).

6. This "deliverance from distress" theme is seen in a few cases of shepherd-king in the ancient Near Eastern texts but other passages were too fragmentary or only epithetical so that a general statement could not be made.

7. The army describes itself as a herd (idr, see Schafer 1905, 87, Line 5; Gardiner 1957, 556; Pritchard 1969, 447d) without herdsman (nn + ptc. Of m[i]niw, see Schafer 1905, 87, line 5; Gardiner 1957, 568; Pritchard 1969, 447d).

8. Ge 30:31; 41:2, 18; Ex 34:3; Isa 11:7; 27:10; 30:23; 65:25; Jer 6:3; Hos 9:2; Jnh 3:7; Job 1:14; 24:21 [Heb.]; SS 2:16; 4:5; and 1 Ch 27:29. Another eighteen uses in non-figurative contexts are without further nuance (Ge 29:9; 30:36; 36:24; 37:2, 12-13, 16; 46:32, 34; 47:3 1 Sa 16:11; 17:15, 34, 40; 2 Ki 10:12; Isa 38:12; and 61:5). Lying down is the activity five times (Isa 11:7; 13:20; 27:10; Zep 2:7; SS 1:7), giving drink four times (Ge 29:7; Ex 2:17, 19; Jnh 3:7), guarding twice (Ge 30:31; Am 3:12), shearing twice (1 Sa 25:7, 16), healing once (figuratively, Isa 30:23); breeding once (Ge 30:25-43) and leading once (Ex 3:1).

9. The use of nāweh makes probable that this is an indication of shepherding activity. Of the 30 uses of nāweh, 26 are certainly dealing with shepherding, or less often animal dwelling and nomadic dwelling, see 2 Sa 7:8; 1 Ch 17:7; Isa 27:10; 32:18 (see v. 16, wilderness and field); 33:20 (tent); 34:13; 35:7; 65:10; Jer 10:21-22 (all their flock, lair of jackals); 23:3 (countries); 25:30 (habitation); 31:23-24 (see v. 24, flocks); 33:12; 49:19–20; 50:7, 19, 44–45; Eze 25:5; 34:14; Ps 79:7 (see v. 13, people as sheep); Job 5:4, 24 (see v. 24, tent); 18:15 (tent); Pr 24:15 (dwelling; see Isa 65:10, place; Jer 50:6, fold).

10. The shepherding activities earlier described are deliverances from distress, but these passages specifically use a salvific word to describe Yahweh's actions toward his sheep.

CHAPTER FOUR

THE METAPHOR OF SHEPHERD
IN THE TORAH

The incomprehensive image of shepherd produced in pastoral theology often takes reference from the New Testament and the priesthood metaphor in the medieval church. Although pastoral theologians justified that the basis is God, it was not followed through and has been replaced by psychology at some points in history.

A careful study will show that it should take reference from God, instead. Shepherding image must come from God, as shall be observed through the history of Israel. God has been very involved in the life of Israel, so much so that he was a shepherd to her. Though God has appointed leaders from time to time, he still provides leadership, protection, and preservation to his leaders, as well as to the community of Israel. However, the image of shepherd in Yahweh is progressive, rather than static. Thus, we must sift through the pages of the Hebrew Bible to understand this image of shepherd. To do this, we shall now turn to Genesis, the first book of the Hebrew Bible.

Genesis

The metaphor of shepherd has been exhibited in the literature of the Hebrew Bible. In Genesis 4:2–3 (NIV), "Later she gave birth to his brother Abel. Now Abel kept flocks, and Cain worked the soil," Gordon Wenham commented that it is an adumbration of the Yahweh's choice work for Abel (1987, 102). It is aligned with the profession of the Patriarchs (Ge 47:3), and the chosen King of Israel, David (1 Sa 16:11). Victor Hamilton (1990, 222) suggested that the profession that which Yahweh assigned to Abel is the traditional profession of the Patriarchs. It is significant because Abel will then walk in the pathway similar to the leaders of Israel such as Jacob (Ge 30:36), Joseph (Ge 37:2), Moses (Ex 3:1), and David (1 Sa 16:11).

What we see in Genesis 4:2–3 is that being a shepherd is a profession with special design in the ancient setting of Genesis, and a pathway to leadership as exemplified by the patriarchs and David. From another perspective, shepherding is not simply a motion of gliding along with the sheep but a process that formatting a leader's characters and skills. Abel, though the Bible did not contain much details of his life, was often perceived as more righteous than his brother, Cain. That us why the verses specially highlighted the profession to reiterate the significance of being a shepherd.

It may be true that shepherding is the ideal profession in the Christian world, but it is not always perceived the same way in the ancient world. In Genesis 46:34 (NIV), shepherds were perceived as "detestable" to the Egyptians. No documentary evidence, however, support this Egyptian attitude (Plaut 1981, 294). Plaut outlined that the Egyptians dislike shepherds can be traced to their historic encounters with Hyksos. The Egyptians understood the term "shepherd" as the same word for "Hyksos." It is more than simply connecting the term to the monarchical status; it is inferred as "foreign rulers" (Plaut 1981, 294).

Speiser argued that the enmity toward shepherds is conjectural. He asserted that this is caused by the interpreted meaning of the word "shepherd" as "shepherd kings" which is abhorrent to the Egyptians at that time (Speiser 1964, 345). Socially, the shepherds are at low strata of the ancient Egyptian society (Sarna 1989, 318). But the context supports that the perspective of shepherd in Egypt is not common in the ancient Near East. The family of Jacob does not know of such connotation to their occupation. Joseph has to instruct his family what they ought to say to Pharaoh when they meet him. Therefore, the disdained identity of shepherds is localized by the Egyptians, rather than popularized in the ancient Near East.

There is an apparent textual contradiction between verse 31, 34a, and 34b of Genesis 46. The Masoretic Text does not contain any further information regarding why the biblical writer scripted it as appeared in the text. One may rely on source criticism for explanation. However, the reason is yet unknown. We may see the inter-textual relationships of these verses in Genesis 46 and that it was the plot of Joseph desiring to procure the land of Goshen for Jacob and his family (Sailhamer 1998, n. 28–34).

Genesis 48:15 brings the direct notion that the title "shepherd" is used at Yahweh. This inference is rare but not inappropriate. According to Sarna, "The image for the deity as a shepherd is common throughout ancient Near Eastern literature and appears frequently in the Bible. It expresses the idea that God as shepherd is the provider, protector, and guide" (Sailhamer 1998, 328). To use the title "shepherd" on Yahweh is to follow the trend of the religious ideology in the times of the ancient Near East.

The context of Genesis 48:8-16 shares insights to our understanding of the title. Yahweh is perceived as the one "before whom my fathers Abraham and Isaac walked" (Ge 48:15 NIV). This has covenant significance in the ancient Near East culture. It implies "loyalty" to the partners in the covenant relationships (Friedman 2001, 157). It also relates to the Aaronic priestly blessings in Numbers 6:24, which also resembles the Babylonian liturgies. The latter, as advocated by Skinner (1930, 506), is a polytheistic practice that the all gods of one's knowledge are named and worshipped. But this proposition is presumptive on Israelites' inference of Yahweh as shepherd. The religion of Israel is monotheistic in nature, and therefore, the relationship with the polytheistic Babylonian liturgical practice is inconclusive. What is established here is the relationship of the shepherd and sheep in the experiences of life as they journeyed through many circumstances. It does play the metaphor of shepherd in the fashion of leading, protecting, and providing for his sheep.

Careful examination of the context may confer a notion to Jacob's understanding of Yahweh. Although it was a common practice in the ancient world to invoke the name of god, it does portray one's understanding of that deity. Jacob, in uttering his words of blessings, invoked that Yahweh, the God who has led him like a shepherd, indicated his understanding of who Yahweh was to him (Ge 48:15). This infers Yahweh's identify to his people, whom he considered as sheep in his fold.

In Genesis 49:24 (NIV), God is referred as "the Shepherd, the Rock of Israel." Keil and Delitzsch (1986, 407) commented that, "God is called 'the Stone,' and elsewhere 'the Rock' (Dt 32:4, 18), as the immoveable [sic] foundation upon which Israel might trust, might stand firm and impregnably secure." This comment relates the shepherd figure to one who saves. Together with the metaphor of shepherd, it portrays that God is a reliable shepherd and is the provider of life. Israelites are supposed to trust in God and embraced this conviction from generation to generation.

Skinner stated that the name "Shepherd" is preferred in Genesis 49:24 (NIV). The Peshitta and Targum of Onkelos are not convincing to infer the meaning. In relation to the name of shepherd, the name "Rock of Israel" is the tribal religious celebration in the ancient Near East (Skinner 1930, 531). Meyer (1906, 282, cited in Skinner 1930, 531, n. 246) added that the name "Rock of Israel" may have a deeper "ancient significance" than if the name is inferred to Yahweh. But the using of the title "Rock" or "Stone" as an epithet is uncommon (Speiser 1964, 369).

Yahweh as "Shepherd" expresses the religious understanding of who God is to Israel, at least in the understanding of Jacob. The context of Genesis 49 is the benedictions of Jacob to his children. In that case, it was to Joseph that Jacob gave these blessings with the invocation of Yahweh's name as "Shepherd." Jacob recognized that Yahweh watched over his people like a shepherd over his sheep. In Joseph's case, Yahweh would watch over him, just as Yahweh watch over Jacob (Ge 49:25).

In summary, we see that Yahweh referred as shepherd is in the trend of the religious practices of the ancient Near East. There is no documentary evidence in support of the remark of Joseph regarding the Egyptians' attitude toward shepherds. Conjectural explanation is plausible but cannot be conclusive. However, Jacob infers Yahweh as shepherd, which is also a religious trend in the ancient Near East. Now that we have observed the shepherd metaphor in Genesis, we shall turn to the shepherd image in Exodus.

Exodus

The Exodus narrative does not contain many evidences pertaining to the shepherd image. In Exodus 3:1, Moses is a shepherd tending the flock of Jethro. This common profession has brought Moses not only an occupation, but also a leadership status. In the ancient Near East culture, the people are inferred as flock to the king. In the Hebrew Bible, it is evidenced that the Israelite leaderships have occupied such profession in their early years (Propp 1999, 221).

Moses as shepherd indicates the dynamism of the implications in the terminology. Propp (1999, 222) stated that,

> The image of the shepherd is polyvalent. Usually it conveys power, authority and concern, as when applied to Yahweh (e.g., Psalm 23). But sometimes it betokens humility and obedience. Often a shepherd does not own his flock, but works for another. By emphasizing that Moses' sheep are actually Jethro's, the text underscores the parallels between Moses' present and future occupations. As he brings Jethro's flock to Horeb, so will he one day bring Yahweh's "flock" to God's mountain.

The comment of Propp on the shepherding profession of Moses expressed the underlying responsibility of leadership designed by Yahweh. It includes leading and bringing the flock to where they belong, and exemplifies with humility and obeisance to the vested commission. It is a multi-facets image.

Being a shepherd also means one is undergoing training for leadership. Peter Enns (2000) understood that the one who assumed the profession as shepherd is indeed in training. Therefore, theologically, Moses undertook shepherding profession because he was training to shepherd God's people (Enns 2000, 95). This is an affirmation to the metaphorical meaning of shepherd in the fashion of leading. It may also infer protecting the people under one's kingship, and providing for the people who are part of the kingdom.

In summary, the shepherd image is rarely expressed in the Exodus narrative, but with evidence of inference to leadership. Religiously, Yahweh equips his leaders through the profession of shepherding, so that they may acquire the skills to lead, provide, and feed the people under their leadership.

Leviticus is the book in the Torah that does not have references to the shepherd metaphor, and that due to the nature of the genre. It is a book that record the levitical rituals for the religion of the ancient Israel. Now that we have observed the shepherd metaphor in Exodus, we shall turn to Numbers to observe the shepherd image.

Numbers

Like the Exodus, the narrative of Numbers does not contain many references regarding the shepherd image. The prominent reference is Numbers 27:17 where Moses replied to Yahweh's judgment against him, and in response, requested for a new leader when he undertook the punishment. The result as in the text, Joshua was chosen by Yahweh to succeed Moses in leading the Israelites to the next lap.

The response of Moses interestingly aware the readers of the responsibility of the shepherd image in the life of the Israelites. The shepherd is to lead his sheep for their entire well-being, and in return, the people shall follow their leader (Plaut 1981, 1204). Its depiction is one of militant traits where the head of the army leads the troops forward and advance to the assigned destination (Budd 1984, 306).

Jacob Milgrom (1989) supported the military traits to say that the verbs are in causative Hifʿil pattern. Also, this verb pattern indicates the responsibility of a military leader is not only to lead the troops, but strategize to win the battle with some establishing of policy (Milgrom 1989, 235). The other example is David in 2 Samuel 5:2 (NIV) where he was commented, "You will shepherd my people Israel, and you will become their ruler." Moses' response to Yahweh is one of selflessness in that he desires the successor to have his caliber, not afraid that he will be eclipsed by the new leader. This characteristic of shepherd leadership may denote an unwavering objective of the shepherd is to ensure the well-being of the sheep, and pass on the scepter into the hands of the replacement shepherd who has the similar objective.

Further textual evidence indicates a strong military trait. The Hebrew here "from coming forth" (yāboʾ) and "and brought them in" (yĕbîʾem) support a military movement. This characteristic includes the military role of divine and human. Baruch A. Levine (2000, 349–350) stated that,

> In the heroic tradition, the God of Israel is said "to go forth" at the heads of Israel's forces to assure them of victory (Judg 4:14, 2 Sam 5:24), whereas the armies, themselves, "go forth" to do battle (Deut 20:1, 21:10, 28:25, 2 Kings

19:9). As a reflex, the Hif'il *hōṣî'* describes the action of a commander, whether divine or human (Isa 40:26, 2 Sam 5:2, 1 Chron 11:2, and see below Num 27:21).

The comment of Levine suited the model of shepherd in Moses. It is, however, necessary to consider the context of pre-monarchy era, in order to understand the significance of the shepherd metaphor in relation to its transition into the monarchical kingship. Therefore, the model of Moses resembles that of the model of a king, which later exhibited in David who is the chosen king of Yahweh.

The shepherd image of Moses is the predecessor of the shepherd image of David. The latter is re-fashioned to suit the political position of a king. Mosaic and Davidic shepherd model are parallel and complementary (Milgrom 1989, 235). Thus, the shepherd metaphor of leadership exhibited in Moses is also expressed in Psalm 77:20 and Isaiah 63:11.

In summary, we see that the narrative of Numbers expresses the pre-monarchy leadership in the shepherd model of Moses. In fact, the shepherd leader image has existed in the early form of human culture, just as the people in the ancient world were perceived as flocks in the fold (Levine 2000, 350). We can conclude that the shepherd leader is a model used in the religion of the ancient Israel, which later developed in its political culture. Now that we have observed the shepherd metaphor in Numbers, we shall turn to observe the shepherd image in Deuteronomy.

Deuteronomy

The narrative of Deuteronomy has no direct reference relating to shepherd metaphor, but it complements the shepherd image in the Pentateuch. Walther Zimmerli (1907) argued that Yahweh has been the shepherd of Israel from the beginning of Israel's history. The experience in Exodus becomes a wilderness experience guided by Yahweh himself. The departure from Egypt has made Israel "a people of hope," as they moved with the shepherding leadership of Yahweh (Zimmerli 1907, 24). This may take reference to the land that Yahweh promised to give, as described in Deuteronomy 12:9–10 (NIV):

> Since you have not yet reached the resting place and the inheritance the LORD your God is giving you. But you will cross the Jordan and settle in the land the LORD your God is giving you as an inheritance, and he will give you rest from all your enemies around you so that you will live in safety.

The context of Deuteronomy 12 is the stipulation of the purpose of the Law given to the Israelites as they possessed the land of promise (Dt 12:1). Yahweh instructed Moses that the Israelites must observe the regulations, and must eradicate the evildoers and the wicked in the land. In so doing, the purifying of the land will stage the placing of Yahweh's name in the land where his people shall dwell (Dt 12:5). Here indicates that one of the fashions of the shepherd image is one who leads the sheep into the land Yahweh promised, protects them by eliminating affliction, and provides them safety from the enemies. Deuteronomy is the finalized version of the mosaic traditions that help the people of Israel to live a life that Yahweh the shepherd has intended, and the other designated shepherds should observe this law code to lead, protect, and provide for the people, who are sheep, to live peacefully in the shepherd fold.

Now that we have observed the shepherd metaphor in Deuteronomy, how shall it relate to the shepherd leadership of Israel? To this, we shall now turn to the next section, the Shepherd Leadership of Israel.

The Shepherd Leadership of Israel

The narratives of Pentateuch expressed the shepherd image prominently in Yahweh and Moses. In Moses' personal shepherding experience, God appointed Moses to be a shepherd to Israel. Moses was born of the tribe of Levite, and later, called to deliver Israel out of the Egyptian bondage. Many people perceived Moses as a leader. Perhaps, another categorization may befit his task, kingship.

Gerhard von Rad (1975, 1: 292) highlighted the role that Moses played in the lives of the Israelites was reasonable to be "an inspired shepherd whom Jahweh used to make known his will." Truly, the shepherding training in Moses' life is a divine deposit preparing him to assume the pastoral leadership of Israel (Ex 3:1). Therefore, the shepherd metaphor manifested in Moses embraces a king/leader figure.

Since Yahweh is the shepherd of Israel, he becomes the great shepherd when he appointed other shepherds to lead his people. These appointed shepherds are accountable to Yahweh for the well-being of the sheep, and thus become mediators between God and their flocks. Moses was one of these appointed shepherds and mediators of the nation Israel. The mediatory role of Moses associated closely to the deliverance of Israel. Moses was both the "mediator of action" and the "mediator of the word." Thus, he embraces a dual role of prophet and priest.

To some degrees, Moses is a prophet. A prophet is one who speaks God's words to the people, and Moses fits that description (Ex 33:11). He prophesied the coming Messiah which eventually, came in the person of Jesus Christ (Dt 18:15). Also, the miraculous signs and wonders that God commanded Moses to perform before the exodus took place and in the wilderness journey (Ex 14:15–22; 17:6; Nu 20:8–11; Dt 34:10–11). Therefore, Moses the prophet, who spoke

God's words to the people, is a mediator of action.

In addition, Moses is also functioning as a priest to the Israelites. Remembered that he was a Levite, of which Yahweh had chosen to set apart for the work of the Tabernacle. But Aaron was chosen to be the priest, and the priesthood in the Hebrew Bible came through him and his descendants. Though Moses was not the chosen priest, he stood in the gap between Yahweh and Israel. A priest is one who intercedes for the community before Yahweh. In many occasions, Moses interceded on behalf of Israel (Ex 32:11–14; Nu 14; Ps 106:23). Through Moses, Yahweh has also established sacrificial and worship order for the entire nation of Israel (Ex 25:9; Lev 7:37–38; Lev 8). Thus, the shepherd leadership of Moses is in his priesthood, and is evident in the Torah.

In his study of Moses, Herbert Wolf remarked that,

> He was a prophet, a priest, and almost a king as he directed every facet of national life. The New Testament highly praises both Abraham and Moses, but it was Moses who appeared on the Mount of Transfiguration, along with Elijah, to talk with Jesus (Matt. 17:3–8). (1991, 47)

Wolf (1991, 49) also described Moses' role during the long forty difficult years in the wilderness as, "their [Israel's] faithful and loyal leader, a skilled shepherd tending his wayward flock." This description depicts Moses was a shepherd and a mediator between Yahweh and Israel; with the function of kingly, priesthood and prophetic responsibility to lead, feed, and protect the people of Israel, Yahweh's sheep.

Significantly, the Exodus narrative coils around the revelation Moses received from Yahweh. Under the revelatory instructions, Moses led the Israelites out of Egypt, through the Red Sea. The interpretation of Moses and the prophets regarding the entire exodus experience are critical to Israel's understanding of the event. Thus, the metaphor of shepherd in the Pentateuch embraces a leadership responsibility, begins with Yahweh himself, and exhibits in his shepherd leader, Moses.

We have observed the shepherd images in the Torah, and the shepherd leadership of Israel based on the shepherd metaphor. There are other studies done on the shepherd image which would be appropriate to mention them here, before proceed further.

Shepherd Image

Further study may be added to the understanding of the shepherd image. For example, Walter Brueggemann took a different approach regarding shepherding imagery. He preferred to use the theme of covenant as the link throughout the revelation of God (Brueggemann 1979, 115–129). Through this covenant theme, Bruggemann drew implications for pastoral care. He employed the term "cove nant," not in its usual meaning used by most Old Testament theologians, but in a metaphorical way. Brueggemann argued that human beings cannot live with freedom apart from the covenant with God, because that is the defined parameter that God would deal with His creation. To him, one must be in covenant relationship with God, and then one can live in freedom. Without covenant, no one can live freely in the world God has created. All implications of the God–given revelation draw from this understanding of the covenant relationship with the creator, and that is also true to pastoral care.

Since Yahweh is the shepherd of Israel, their relationship is undoubtedly close. God as shepherd displays the quality of fatherly love to His children. To this regard, R.S. Sunderland (1981) explained that God loves and exercises discipline over His children, Israel. This is further shown in Deuteronomy 28:1–68, where God outlines the condition of blessings and disciplinary actions (Sunderland 1981, 34). This may help us to understand the significance of the Law given through Moses at Mount Sinai.

Law is often seen as rigid regulations aim to control the life of people. Israel is not immune to this misconception and fails to appreciate God's good intention. A careful study of the Law would help one to see the purpose of the Law. Mark Strom (1990, 52) commented that the Law is set to guide Israel in her relationship with God, and that Israel needs to know how to live as covenant people in the presence of God. This is critical to Israel as sheep; she needs to obey the guidance of Yahweh, her shepherd. Without law, one may go astray and abuse the freedom that God has bestowed upon us. Therefore, law is to guide us back to the pathway that God has intended us to sojourn.

The shepherding imagery in the Pentateuch is derived from the intervention of Yahweh in the life of the Israelites. He is the source of leadership, protection and provision of life embraced with love (Ge 49:24; see Ge 48:15). Yahweh as the shepherd of Israel is to bring the people to the promised land. Since the promise was made long ago, the shepherding responsibility of God may be to fulfill his covenant promise to Abraham (Zimmerli 1907, 30). The other designated shepherds simply act in according to the pattern that Yahweh has set before them, and carry on with the same objective.

In summary, we have observed the shepherd metaphor in the torah, and despite only Genesis has most references regarding the metaphor, the entire first division of the Hebrew Bible depicts the imagery in a refined fashion for readers to grapple with the significance of the shepherd image. The metaphor of Yahweh as shepherd begins in Torah and also exhibited in other parts of the Hebrew Bible. To proceed further, we shall now turn to the metaphor of shepherd in the Former Prophetic literature.

CHAPTER FIVE

THE METAPHOR OF SHEPHERD IN THE FORMER PROPHETIC LITERATURE

The metaphor of shepherd in the former prophetic literature begins at the closing of Mosaic era to the monarchical period. However, the metaphor takes a different course and it is exhibited through the judges, prophets, priests, and kings. We shall now turn to the metaphor of shepherd from Moses to the Judges.

The Metaphor of Shepherd from Moses to the Judges

The shepherding role of God continues from the Torah to the Former Prophetic literature. After the leadership of Moses, incidental shepherd leaders arose in Israel until the rise of Samuel. Joshua, though a leader, he was more a conqueror than a shepherd. He might have exhibited the shepherd figure of leading. In the period of Judges, God had raised many judges as leaders only to respond to the cries of the Israelites to deliver them from the oppression of the enemies. They, however, may exhibit the shepherd image of protecting the sheep.

The shepherding image in the Former Prophetic literature expresses in a different form. After the era of Joshua, Israel established the priesthood system and it became the core of their religious life. At that time, the religious practices of Israelites became cultic, in the sense that, "Their daily duties consisted of offer–

ing sacrifices (Deut 33:10), pronouncing blessings (Num 6:22–27) and maintaining moral, physical and social purity" (Tidball 1986, 42). This spells out a new era in the history of ancient Israel. However transient the leadership of Judges was, it displayed a picture of deliverance from Yahweh the shepherd through his designated shepherd, who performed the same function of protecting the sheep. This is, as discussed earlier, a fashion of shepherd metaphor in protecting the flock. With the newly established system of priesthood, the shepherd metaphor took a different form. To this, we now turn to the metaphor of shepherd in priesthood.

The Metaphor of Shepherd in Priesthood

Unlike the Judges in the previous era, Samuel has multiple roles. He was "a judge, priest and prophet," and this supported a facet of the shepherd metaphor exhibited in Yahweh and Moses. However, these offices are in no sense contradictory to each other, and not even to the shepherd image. The writers of the New Testament considered Samuel as a prophet (Ac 3:24), and it was probably the reason as in the pre-monarchical period that Yahweh's word "was rare" (1 Sa 3:1 NIV). Truly, through the prophetic pattern of Eli, Samuel learnt the religious customs, "Speak, LORD, for your servant is listening" (1 Sa 3:9-10 NIV).

Although Samuel was not a shepherd, he was a leader at his time. His unitary figure of priesthood and prophet in the metaphor of shepherd expressed the shepherd fashion of leading, providing, and feeding in a different way. In the monarchical period, the role of the judge was no longer needed as Yahweh had set kings to rule Israel. As priests, one of their responsibilities is to offer sacrifices to Yahweh for the community. They lead the people in the way of Yahweh. They are to stand in the gap between God and man; as a mediator is part of their shepherd role in providing peace and securing well-being, by mediating for the people (see 2 Sa 15:27–28).

At times, priests will pass instructions to the people of Israel apart from the usual guidance according to the Laws (2 Ki 11:15–16). The passing of instructions in the role of the priest is to inquire of Yahweh on behalf of the king and the community of Israel, which often is what the king will request before making any decision. What Yahweh says, the priests will convey to the king, and sometimes in the form of an oracle (e.g., 2 Ch 20:14–17.). An example of such proclamation of blessing or curse through Yahweh's word can be found in Haggai 2:11–14. In verse 11–12 (NIV), the prophet begins with the directive of Yahweh:

"This is what the LORD Almighty says: 'Ask the priests what the law says: If a person carries consecrated meat in the fold of his garment, and that fold touches some bread or stew, some wine, oil or other food, does it become consecrated?'" The priests answered, "No."

The prophet continues his inquisition:

> Then Haggai said, "If a person defiled by contact with a dead body touches one
> of these things, does it become defiled?" "Yes," the priests replied, "it becomes
> defiled."

According to the Laws, the priest must answer with an emphatic definite "de-
filed" (Hag 2:13 NIV). What comes next is a judgment of God pronounced by
the prophet to the Israelites (Hag 2:14 NIV);

> Then Haggai said, "'So it is with this people and this nation in my sight,' de-
> clares the LORD. 'Whatever they do and whatever they offer there is defiled.

The point in this incident is that Yahweh's word is the directive power and the
prophet is the instrument for a directive purpose. To add, the directive power of
the priests is a fashion of leading, providing, and feeding figures of the shepherd
image. The priest, such as Samuel, leads the people to live in the desires of
Yahweh, provides spiritual guidance to the people, so that they may do according to the desires of Yahweh, and feeds the social community with the religious
instructions of Yahweh transmitted to the people via the words of a priest, but
not in terms of physical food. Thus, the role of a priest embraces the full sphere
of shepherd metaphor in the royal court of the nation of Israel, as well as in the
religious and social life of the Israelites.

The function of priesthood has developed progressively in Israel's history.
Only in Moses, and perhaps, Samuel, we see the full shepherding metaphor as
mediator in the roles of a priest, prophet, judge and may be, king or leader. The
last of these roles is an ancient appellation subscribed in association with the
title "shepherd" (Brettler 1989).

Like Moses, priests are mediators in the narrative of Pentateuch and in the
Monarchical period. Therefore, the function of priestly mediation can be traced
back to the traditions contained in the Pentateuch (Ex 28; Dt 33:8).

Though the king is the leader of the nation, the responsibility of teaching
the Laws falls on the shoulder of the priests (2 Ch 17:7-9). Haggai 2:11–13 fur-
nishes a vivid example of Torah instructions. Zimmerli (1907, 97) writes, "The
priest is the expert protector of these distinctions, who instructs people, for example, in the 'rules that ensure life' (Ezek 33:15) to be observed by anyone who
enters the Holy Place." Also, some priests are appointed as judges in Jerusalem
under the supervision of the chief priest (2 Ch 19:8–11). Although this role of
priesthood is rare, its origin comes from the priesthood in the Pentateuch. In
Deuteronomy 17:8–13, the Laws stipulated a judicial sanction for the priests to
act as judges. To this regard, Zimmerli (1907, 98) outlined that:

> According to the evidence of Exodus 22:7–8, the sanctuary becomes involved
> in the legal process only to clear up crimes that would otherwise go unex

plained. Deuteronomy 31:9ff and 27:14ff speak of solemn legal proclamations before the assembled community in which the Levites play an important role. But the full involvement of the priests in legal transactions is probably best ascribed to the period when Israel ceased to be an independent state.

Ezekiel 44:24 (NIV) outlines the ordinance of the priesthood that which includes serving as a judge, to instruct the people on the Laws and to "keep my Sabbaths holy." An interesting aspect of mediatory role of the priesthood is to bless the people of God. This expresses the providing of safety in the shepherd image.

Priests in the monarchical period also functioned as wise men. Probably, they were the ones who had left their wise instructions in the wisdom literature in the Christian canonical order. These priests who are wise men may be referred to as "political counselors in the government" (Zimmerli 1907, 107). The story of revolt by Absalom shows the critical role of counselor in relation to the future of the nation (2 Sa 17:14). Wrong counsel will bring disaster, while wise counsel will align with the desires of Yahweh, and bring prosperity to the nation. More so, it shows the participation of Yahweh in the royal council. For example, the accounts of Solomon's wise leadership in the case of the two women (1 Ki 3:16-28; see 1 Ki 3:12). Yahweh answered Solomon's request by giving him "a wise and discerning heart" to resolve the maternal conflict (1 Ki 3:12; 3:28 NIV). Through the God-given wisdom, Solomon was able to establish peace with surrounding nations and bring prosperity to the nation of Israel (1 Ki 5:9–14; 10:1–13).

These wise men function as shepherd in providing wise guidance that is essential to the well-being of the nation of Israel. The ideal character is Solomon, who is a wise king. He has truly exhibited the shepherd image in that, first, he is a king to his people, as shepherd to the sheep, and second, a wise man, provides security in his wise decision. Thus, the shepherd image exhibited in the role of wise men is to lead people with discernment, feed them with the justice of Yahweh, and protect them with wisdom (1 Ki 3:12, 28).

Lastly, in 1 Chronicles 23:28–31, the priests' responsibility is to mediate for the people daily with thanks and praises to the Lord. Through that mediation process, and when God finds favor in the people, blessings shall flow from Yahweh to his people. This was conspicuous in the instructions given to the priests in Deuteronomy 10:8 (cf. Nu 6:22–27). Here, the priest in the metaphor of shepherd in the figure of providing security is to bless the people of Yahweh. This truly expresses an aspect of the shepherd metaphor. Now that we have observed the metaphor of shepherd in priesthood, we shall turn to the metaphor of shepherd in kingship.

The Metaphor of Shepherd in Kingship

The Former Prophetic narratives, though recorded many heroic characters, one must mention the great king of Israel, a shepherd in the initial training, the chosen king of Yahweh, the son of Jesse, David. He is the focal point of the history of Israel.

In 1 Samuel 16:11, Samuel visited Jesse and his family by the order of Yahweh to appoint a new king. David was not in the house as he was shepherding his father's flocks, when Samuel arrived and previewed the potential royal candidates. The texts of 1 Samuel 17:15 supported the evidence of David's profession in the early days; he was a shepherd boy. The role of shepherd image in providing security is prescribed in 1 Samuel 17:34–35 (NIV),

> But David said to Saul, "Your servant has been keeping his father's sheep.
> When a lion or a bear came and carried off a sheep from the flock, I went after
> it, struck it and rescued the sheep from its mouth. When it turned on me, I
> seized it by its hair, struck it and killed it.

Implicitly, the description of David to Saul regarding his work, while he was a shepherd, aligned his shepherd image of providing for security, apart from leading from pasture to pasture, and feeding the sheep. Parallel to David, Moses protected the Israelites from the Egyptians, and Samuel provided spiritual direction to the people of Israel.

In his battle with Goliath in 1 Samuel 17:40, David fought with shepherd skills reminded us of his professional training as a shepherd of his father's flock. The normal weapon in battlefield is sword. In 1Samuel 17:39, we see that David was not accustomed to the usual battle attire and weapon, and decided on his shepherd sling. He was confident in what he was trained. Perhaps, David imagined himself fighting for the survival of his flock, as he was about to approach Goliath. The shepherding training not only trained David in skills but also imparting passion toward his flock, in this case, the people of Israel. This is the dynamism of the shepherding role.

The explicit reference to David as king of Israel is in 2 Samuel 5:2 (NIV),

> In the past, while Saul was king over us, you were the one who led Israel on
> their military campaigns. And the LORD said to you, 'You will shepherd my
> people Israel, and you will become their ruler.'"

This is the promulgation of kingship succession. It is not difficult to realize that the kingship is inferred, by the phrase, "will shepherd my people." The ancient Near Eastern culture perceived the king as shepherd, and being part of this culture, Israel understood this convention well. The responsibilities of a king was widely resembles that of a shepherd image in the ancient Near East convention (Baldwin 1988, 194). On the parallel, the understanding of shepherd in the Old Testament literature is in almost similar light. Yahweh is shepherd to Israel in the sense that he cares for them and provides protection (Ge 49:24). Baldwin

(1988, 194–195) states that,

> The consciousness that the Lord was the shepherd of Israel (Pss 23; 74:1;
> 77:20; 78:52; 80:1; 95:7) meant that Israel's human shepherds had before them
> the highest possible model of faithfulness, justice and loving kindness. By their
> exercise of these qualities they were judged.

There is no certainty that the ancient Near Eastern literature denotes the king in
a manner similar to the Israelites. Here, as Yahweh is shepherd of Israel is to
lead with certain characteristics, not only in aptitude. His flock will determine a
good shepherd by these characteristics. Likewise, the human ruler or shepherd
who is considered good must exemplify these characteristics.

In relation to kingship, the covenant relationship Yahweh is established
with Israel through its leaders or shepherds. Perhaps, Yahweh foresees the potential tyrannical attitude of a king, he formulates the covenant agreement to
prevent the abuse of the royal authority (1 Sa 8:10–18). But at the same time, the
people under the kingship should ensure "their royalty support" (Baldwin 1988,
195).

It is an honor to be a shepherd in the ancient Near East. Deities and humans
who are considered as shepherd received similar honor, and this is found in the
lists of Sumerian kings, in the style of Babylonian court, and the pyramid texts,
which are the books of the dead, and these have been followed throughout the
ancient Near Eastern culture (Beyreuther 1978, 564). Compatibly, the literature
of the ancient Near Eastern and the Hebrew Bible affirmed that the significance
of kingship is associated with shepherd, and particularly, in the literature of the
Hebrew Bible, Yahweh is the divine shepherd, and David is the human shepherd
to the people of Israel.

The Hebrew here in 2 Samuel 5:2 (NIV) translated as "led" refers not only
to military activities but also that of the military officer (Anderson 1989, 75).
This describes the military ruler leads the troop in and out of their base when
engage in battle. Religiously, the god is a shepherd to his people in the ancient
Near Eastern world. This understanding has been transmitted to the national life
of Israel, as well (Anderson 1989, 76).

Interestingly, in the literature of the Hebrew Bible, Yahweh is called as
shepherd, compared to the ancient Near Eastern literature (Ge 49:24; Ps 23:1;
80:2 [1 NIV]; see Ge 48:15). He is often depicted as the shepherd of Israel (Isa
40:11; see Ps 23:3; Isa 49:10) (Anderson 1989, 76). More interestingly, the
kings of Judah and Israel were not named as "shepherd," but rather the other
national leaders, present and future (Ps 78:71; Jer 3:15; 23:4; Eze 34:23; Eze
37:24). However, Schmidt (1970, 124, cited in McCarter 1984, 132) argued that
the verb rāʿāh "Shepherd," in the narratives of Samuel through Kings is used to
mean "rule." This observation indicates that though the governing system of
Israel in the rule of Yahweh is different, it is not insulated from the influence of
the ancient Near Eastern culture. The culture of Israel is somewhat influenced

by the surrounding ancient Near Eastern conventions.

The relationship between the shepherd and the sheep is intimate. The shepherd leads and the sheep follow. When the shepherd is dead, the sheep is despair. First Kings 22:17 (RSV),

> Then Micaiah answered, "I saw all Israel scattered on the hills like sheep without a shepherd, and the LORD said, 'These people have no master. Let each one go home in peace,'"

signifies that the defeated Israel will be like sheep without a shepherd, because their master is dead (DeVries 1985, 268). Likewise, the life and safety of the sheep depends on the shepherd. Thus, Yahweh as shepherd is the protector of his sheep, and so are all his appointed shepherds over the people of Israel. Now that we have observed the metaphor of shepherd in kingship, we shall turn to the metaphor of shepherd in prophetic office.

The Metaphor of Shepherd in Prophetic Office

Not only the priesthood and kingship are related to the shepherd image, the prophetic office also shares the shepherding responsibility. The prophetic office is not hereditary, unlike the priesthood and kingship. In 1 Kings 19:16, God revealed to Elijah that he would be succeeded by Elisha, and that revelation is a specific appointment of an individual to assume the prophetic office.

Prophets are forbidden to say more than or subtract what God has spoken through them (Dt 18:20; 1 Ki 20:13–14; and Jer 26:2), neither should they mix with their personal words of wisdom. As mentioned in the previous section, the shepherding role of Moses has prophetic responsibility to speak Yahweh's words to his people; Moses did not add or subtract from the divine directives. Another aspect of the shepherd image pertaining to the prophetic office is the prophetic authority. Although this should rightly belong to the next chapter, it may be appropriate to discuss briefly here.

Prior to the writing prophets, prophets were accompanied by the spirit of God, somewhat similar to a deliver, or judge, or the king. Zimmerli (1907, 101) added to say that, it "refers to a dynamistic phenomenon emanating from Yahweh that seizes the prophets and impels him to do things that would be impossible in rational everyday life." Yahweh inspires his appointed shepherds to perform task that would have been difficult to ordinary leaders. This is simply because the role of the shepherd is to provide protection to the sheep, but without divine power, security is lost. As shepherd, Yahweh protects his people, so also the prophet as shepherd, acts as deliverer or judge to the people. Therefore, Yahweh bestows extraordinary power to the prophets, so that they may perform according to their assigned tasks.

The word "spirit" or power of God is not the only expression accompanying the prophetic office, because at times, it is understood in its literal meaning, "the hand of Yahweh" (lit., yad yĕhwāh), that come upon the prophets, instead (1 Ki 18:46; cf. 2 Ki 3:15–16.). The New International Version of the Bible translates yad yĕhwāh as the "hand of God" in 2 Kings 3:15–16, perhaps attempt to highlight the dynamistic nature of Yahweh's hand, which is the miraculous power that empowers the prophet Elisha. It depicts not a form of transcendent influence, but the laying of a physical hand somewhat similar to human hands, except that is from Yahweh. Furthermore, Edmund Jacob (1958, 242–243) says that,

> It is not only through his sight and his feelings that the prophet knows God, his whole being is seized by God; very often we read that Yahweh's hand seizes the prophet (Isa.8:11; Jer.15:17; Ezek.3:14) or that the spirit taken possession of him, making him into an ish haruach (Hos.9:7), so that sometimes he finds that he is outside himself in a state of ecstasy, which can be manifested as abnormal excitement, or on the other hand by a state verging on apathy. (See 1 Kgs 18:12–46, 2 Kgs 2:16; and Jer 29:26)

Thus, indicates that the "Spirit" or the "hand of Yahweh" expressed the empowering act from Yahweh to his prophets, his shepherds.

The function of the prophetic office is also similar to the traditional mode of seer (1 Sa 9:9). Gad, the prophet is mentioned as "David's seer" when the word of God came upon him (2 Sa 24:11; 1 Ch 21:9; 29:29 NIV). Samuel who has multiple roles is also called a "seer" (1 Ch 9:22; 26:28; 29:29 NIV). Another example is Jehu who is known as "seer" to Jehoshaphat, king of Judah (2 Ch 19:2 NIV). The seers provide direction and guidance to the king of Israel. Although the king is a shepherd to the people, the seers function as shepherds to the king in the sense that they are engaged in the planning of the peoples' welfare and strategizing for war with the peace of the people in mind.

We, so far, have observed the shepherd image in the prophets served in the royal courts. There is a group of prophets, who are serving the public. These prophets have a greater obligation, especially to the nation of Israel, and not just within the king's court. Elijah and Elisha are the prominent figures of this type of prophet.

The main role of the public prophets is to be covenant reminders. They are to remind the people of Israel to observe the covenant, which God has made with them, so that they will not sin against God. The covenant relationship is build upon the shepherd and the sheep. The prophets lead the people to walk the right path to do good, and feed them with the truths they received from Yahweh for the spiritual growth of the people. Thus, the shepherd image of the public prophets is leading people to the righteous path, feeding with the covenant of Yahweh, so that to protect them from disaster.

In summary, the shepherd image in the monarchical period displays in the facets of priest, prophet and king is established to lead, protect and feed the na tion of Israel, the sheep, for the development of their faith through the instruction of the Laws and the reminding of the covenant. On the parallel, in the Torah, Yahweh and Moses are shepherds to the Israelites. At the same time, Aaronic priesthood, which is the predecessor of the priesthood in the monarchical period, is also vested with the responsibility of a shepherd. As the shepherd leadership of Moses phasing out, God assigns the shepherding role to Joshua, the appointed judges, Samuel and the human kings of Israel. We shall see more of the shepherding role of the priests and prophets in the Latter Prophetic literature. To that, we shall now turn to the metaphor of shepherd in the Latter Prophetic literature to understand the metaphor more fully through the expressed words of the prophets.

CHAPTER SIX

THE METAPHOR OF SHEPHERD IN
THE LATTER PROPHETIC LITERATURE

As mentioned earlier in the Former Prophetic literature, the prophetic office is one of the facets of the shepherd metaphor. This characteristic is evident in the writings of the prophets. Remember, the earlier observation on the role of the prophetic office is one who is a covenant reminder. It is a mediatory role to remind the people of Yahweh to keep the covenant, distinct from the role of a priest, who calls the people to observe the Law. Both roles are important to the spiritual well-being and covenant relationship with Yahweh.

William S. LaSor, David A. Hubbard and Frederic W. Bush (1982) outlined that the prophet and prophetic message embraced the national life of Israel. The prophetic message highlights the unjust and unrighteous practices of every level of leadership, both public and domestic. They include the idolatrous king, the false prophets, the irresponsible priests, unethical merchants, the unjust judges, and the "greedy women." One way of shepherding is that Yahweh gives words to his prophet to speak to the earthly ruler of his people, so that they may know how to lead the people.

Prophetic message is judgment words from Yahweh to Israel because Israel needs to repent from wickedness and return to Yahweh's instructions, so that they may not incur judgment upon themselves. This message of repentance is based on the covenant relationship with Yahweh and thus, true followers of Yahweh envisaged hope through the prophetic message that encompassed the "redemptive purpose" of Yahweh (LaSor, Hubbard and Bush 1982, 305). There-fore, the prophetic office is critical to the rise and fall of the nation of Israel. Though it seems to concern only the political well-being, it has a spiritual im-pact to the social and national life of the Israelites.

In relation to the role of a covenant reminder, prophets are shepherds to Is-rael. LaSor, Hubbard and Bush (1982) commented that the prophetic message assigned to the prophets is both present and proleptic. It does speak to the cur-rent situation of Israel, but also to the ultimate plan Yahweh has in mind. In this way, the people of Israel have hope through the prophetic message, and have courage to move forward into the future. The messages are designed to fulfill Yahweh's purpose through the historical events in Israel's present situation, yet encompassed within the mandate of Yahweh's redemptive purpose (LaSor, Hubbard, and Bush 1982, 305).

LaSor, Hubbard, and Bush also added that the prophetic message position as a tread of redemption to the people of Israel. The message speaks through the prophet is relevant to the political situation, though with spiritual overtone. With this spiritual note, the prophet ushers the people to the plan of Yahweh, and they are inspired by his acts and focus on the truth that emits from the mouth of the prophet (LaSor, Hubbard, and Bush 1982, 305). In this sense, the prophet pro-vides spiritual guidance to their flock, which may be equivalent to Paul's doc-trine of the Scriptures; that is, "for teaching, rebuking, correcting and training in righteousness" (2 Tim 3:16 NIV).

LaSor, Hubbard and Bush (1982) further added that prophecy is an arena where Yahweh's acts would be understood by his people through his prophets, that otherwise would be incomprehensible. Details may not be comprehensive to the level of one's satisfaction, but it will be explicated in the future and is pro-gressive. Yahweh utilizes prophecy to transmit the future of humanity into words or declaration. People who hear these prophetic words from the prophets should then know how to respond to the anticipated outcome, and that is what Yahweh expects his people to do (LaSor, Hubbard and Bush 1982, 305).

It is in this chapter that we shall observe the shepherd image exhibited in the Latter Prophetic literature in details. Let us first observe the prophecy of Isaiah.

Isaiah

The prophetic literature of Isaiah consists of shepherd image, particularly, in the section on the Servant Songs (Isa 40–57). Tidball (1986, 49) outlined that the chapters 40–66 shove the discourse of Yahweh's revelation to a climax beyond any prophets and visions, including Isaiah. He expresses the unfathomable thoughts in magnificent poetic manner. In no sense, Isaiah is attempting to dis-play his academic aptitude, or contributing to the academia of his day. He only speaks with pastoral concerns over the people of Israel.

These opinions present an overview of the theology embraced by the prophet, but his writings show more. Bullock affirmed that the writings in these chapters indicated that Isaiah is embraced by comfort as he penned them. Unlike the previous section on chapters 1–39, Isaiah was burdened by the judgment words of Yahweh that filled with confusion and failure (Bullock 1986, 147). This section, chapters 40–66, emanates a sense of joy over the forthcoming redemption.

Yahweh as Shepherd is to protect His sheep. Bullock highlighted that the theology of Isaiah emerged in the expression of the enmity between Yahweh and his sinful people. The refusal of repentance is the core of the political disaster that which Isaiah sternly believed, theologically, as the pitfall of the theocratic nation of Israel. Israel should only have confidence in Yahweh, and not in earthly foreign political alliances. All these underlie in the significance of Yahweh as the Holy One of Israel, antagonized by the rebellious Israel in chapters 1–39, and the same Holy One of Israel is anticipated to be the redeemer (Bullock 1986, 155–156).

Here, Isaiah urged the nation of Israel to a covenant renewal with her God, Yahweh. This is simply because the sheep will be lost without a shepherd. By not remaining within the covenant relationship, Israel will be devoured and lost forever. In the covenant relationship, it means also to enjoy the blessings of Yahweh. Only in the covenant relationship, can Israel be saved because they are in their shepherd's arm. In the shepherd image of protecting, the shepherd figure is associated with the deliverance of Israel, and theologically, to its redemption.

We have so far observed the shepherd image in the overview of the prophetic literature of Isaiah. However, a meticulous examination of the texts may help us to appreciate the shepherd image in this prophetic literature of Isaiah.

In Isaiah 40:11, the reference to shepherd may be related to Psalm 23:1. However, the image here is one with "royal overtones" because the king is inferred as shepherd as in the ancient Near Eastern culture (Watts 1987, 90). The people of God are expressed in the pictures of flock, lambs, and ewes. The context of Isaiah 40:11 indicates that the Judean city was devastated in the reign of the foreign rule. The return of Yahweh in the future precludes the assurance of the shepherd's leadership, protection, and provision, especially to those in destitute (Watts 1987, 90). Further to note is the term "his bosom" (ḥēyqó) denotes that the fold which the shepherd extended to the flock is for shelter (Watts 1987, 90). This depicts the image of protection in the shepherd metaphor.

The shift from kingly to shepherd metaphor points to the Davidic image (see 2 Sa 5:2; 7:7–8, Mic 5:3 [Masoretic Text]; Eze 34:23–24). Isaiah 40:11 denotes the care of a shepherd toward the sheep. Motyer (1993, 302) outlines the care of the shepherd in the text. "Tends" (NIV, rāʿāh) is care to the needs ("gathers the lambs" NIV, yĕqabbēṣ ṭĕlāʾîm) of the people in the general sense. "Carries them close to his heart" (ûbĕḥēyqó íśśā) with his "arms" (NIV, zĕrōʿó) indicate how the shepherd cares for the sheep. "Close to his heart" (NIV, ûbĕḥēyqó) also indicates intimate relationship between the shepherd and the sheep. Delitzsch (1969, 2:146–147) asserted that the people of Israel is like flock that needs care from their shepherd, Yahweh. We see that all the above descriptions fit the Davidic kingship, and it is in David, we see Yahweh rules Israel, just as a shepherd lead, protect, and feed the sheep.

The kings in the history of Israel are assigned by Yahweh to shepherd his people, regardless they are domestic or foreign rulers. Cyrus is one example. In Isaiah 44:28, Yahweh appointed Cyrus to be his shepherd, and fulfilled his plan. It is interesting to realize that Cyrus is a foreign king, yet Yahweh appoints him to build Jerusalem (2 Ch 36:23). The stress here is the pronoun "my," because the rest of the verse clings on it. Watts (1987, 156) stated that the word "accomplish" (yašlim) shares the same root as peace and "purpose" (Isa 44:28 NIV, "please," ḥēpeṣ) refers to the will of Yahweh. This observation highlights the restoration of Jerusalem lies in the appointment of Cyrus, a foreign king, and the reign of Babylon over Israel.

Information regarding Cyrus is scarce in the Hebrew Bible, and Isaiah 44:28 is significant especially to his role in the history of Israel. The prophetic literature recorded Cyrus as a shepherd, the commonly inferred title of a king in the world of the Hebrew Bible and the ancient Near East. It is also a title inferred to Yahweh. Thus, Cyrus may be considered as Israelite king, in that respect (McKenzie 1968, 73).

To say that Cyrus is an Israelite king is metaphorical, not literal, but certainly, he is Yahweh's servant. We see that Yahweh shepherd his people Israel through a foreign shepherd, Cyrus, who will fulfill his plan. The appointment of Cyrus indicates that Yahweh is a greater shepherd than any earthly shepherd he has appointed. He has not only the power to appoint shepherds from among his people Israel, but also from the surrounding nations.

The responsibility of shepherd concerns the future of the sheep, just as a king to the future of his nation. When the shepherd leadership is absent, the nation of Israel is in ruin. For example, Isaiah 56:11 indicates that not only the enemies of Israel preyed over it, the shepherds have "lack understanding" (NIV, lō᾽ yādʿū hābîn) to lead and guard Jerusalem. These foolish shepherds followed their own desires, and disobeyed Yahweh's instructions, turning from right to wrong (Watts 1987, 257). It is further indicated in the phrase "all turn to their own way" (NIV, kullām lĕdarkām) that these wicked shepherds satisfied themselves to their "own gain" (NIV, ᾽îš lĕbiṣʿô miqqāṣēhû), on the sheep (see Delitzsch 1969, 367). The foolish and irresponsible shepherds are selfish to look after their own well-being, instead of protecting the sheep. Probably, these shepherds are the national leaders of Israel, and in time of wars, they preyed on the sheep. This is due to their lack of knowledge of Yahweh's instructions to know what is right, and thus, they commit wrongdoings. They lack the sensitivity to the apparent needs of the sheep (Motyer 1993, 469).

The word "gain" (NIV, beṣaʿ) indicates a deeper meaning of the shepherds' selfishness. It is used in a negative sense, perhaps gaining by forced possession,

and unable to differentiate right from wrong decisions. Motyer (1993, 469) added that the Hebrew "each man" ('iš) indicates that these shepherds are indulged
totally in seeking for their own profits. This may cause devastation to the nation
of Israel.

In Isaiah 63:11, Moses the servant of Yahweh was mentioned in partnership
with Yahweh, assisting the Israelites crossing the Red Sea. However, this act
was done in the power of the great shepherd, Yahweh. The phrase "he who
brought   them   through   the   sea"   (NIV,   'ammô 'aîyēh
hamma'ālem miyām' indicates that Moses was the one referred in the passage.
The term "shepherd" (NIV, rō'ēy, "shepherds") in qal participle masculine plu-
ral absolute may either refer to Moses, Aaron, and Yahweh (Watts 1987, 332;
Motyer 1993, 515). Delitzsch (1969, 458) stated that with the word "shepherds,"
the conjecture that Moses was inferred became invalid. Watts (1987, 332) suggested that the "shepherds" may refer to the Israelite leaders during the exodus.
But this does not quench the curiosity toward the identity of the "shepherds."

A careful examination of the text indicates that Yahweh is the one "who
brought them through the sea" (NIV, 'aîyēh hamma'ālem miyām). The context
tells us that Isaiah recounting the magnificent works of Yahweh from the old
days. Isaiah 63:11 describes the event of Israel crossing the Red Sea. Here, the
exegesis comes into fruition. First, Yahweh is the one who rescues the Israelites
out of the sea. The context of the Exodus event affirms it. Second, the "shepherds" may refer to the leaders of the Israelites (so Watts), since the next phrase
"of his flock" (NIV, ṣō'nô) suggests that the flock belongs to a third party, and
that is Yahweh, as suggested by the masculine singular pronoun, and the reference to the "his holy Spirit." However, with "his flock" (NIV) may lead us to
conclude that the "shepherds" could have referred to Moses and Aaron (Motyer
1993, 514–515). Therefore, Yahweh as shepherd of Israel, though assigned
earthly shepherds to lead, protect, and feed his people, he is the one great shepherd who leads his people out of slavery from Egypt.

The context of crossing the Red Sea continues through to Isaiah 63:13–14.
The phrase, "who led them through the depths?" (NIV, môlîkām batthōmôt)
speaks of Yahweh, as interpreted within the context of Isaiah 63. Once again,
Yahweh performs his shepherding role leading his sheep, Israel, in the wilderness (bammidbār). The next phrase "they did not stumble" (NIV, lō' ikkāšēlû)
suggests that the image of "providential leading" in the Exodus event (Watts
1987, 333). Motyer (1993, 515) supported that the care of the shepherd, Yahweh, is great, and that the sheep could journey through the bare land.

It is clear that Yahweh is the one inferred in Isaiah 63:13 who did his shepherding duty. The Hebrew "walk" (hālak) indicates that Yahweh walked with
his people through the wilderness with care, and that is why they did not stumble. This is the shepherd image of leading and providing for the sheep in the
journey, and also, protecting by delivering them from their enemies, as affirmed
in the context of the Exodus experience recollected in Isaiah 63:11–14.

Isaiah 63:14 further explicates the shepherd image exhibited in Yahweh.

The entering to the land of Canaan signifies the provision of rest (nûaḥ) in the pasture (see Watts 1987, 333). Although feeding the pasture is the normal routine, the shepherd, Yahweh leads his sheep, Israel, to rest in Canaan (Motyer 1993, 515). Delitzsch (1967, 459) pictured the sheep after a hard day traveling through the barren land come at rest in the richness of a new pasture.

The imagery here is pertaining to the shepherding activity of leading, feeding, and providing rest. Yahweh shepherd Israel in spirit according to the interpretation of Isaiah to the event (Isa 63:14). Although there are earthly shepherds among the Israelites, Yahweh is the one who ensures that his flock has rested. This is the metaphor of shepherd in leading, feeding, and providing rest, as an act of protecting the sheep that come under his pastoral care.

In the understanding of the shepherd image in the above observation, as a prophet, Isaiah assumed the shepherd image and responsibility. He involved God into the picture with a plea that Israel needs to return to Yahwistic worship and belief system, and at the same time, prophesy about another shepherding figure to come in the future. As a shepherd, Isaiah has compassion over Israel, and he desired them to return to Yahweh. He stood as a mediator to bring the Israelites back to the covenant relationship, so that they might not incur the judgment of God; it is a metaphor of shepherd in leading and protecting.

To summarize, the prophetic literature contains metaphorical images of Yahweh as shepherd, as well as Moses and Cyrus, exhibited in the history of Israel. The national leaders of the present and the tribal leaders of the past did function as shepherds to the people of Israel. The significance is the critical role a shepherd plays in building the nation with the instructions of Yahweh, or destroying the nation by his/her own selfish desires. In other words, the life of the nation of Israel, community, or flock lies in quality of its shepherd leadership. Now that we have observed the shepherd metaphor in the prophetic literature of Isaiah, we shall turn to the prophetic literature of Jeremiah.

Jeremiah

There are significant biblical references pertaining to the image of shepherd in the prophetic literature of Jeremiah. Like Isaiah, a careful examination of the Hebrew text of Jeremiah will explicate the metaphor more vividly.

In Jeremiah 3:15, Yahweh promised to send shepherds who followed his model, and urged Israel to return to him. The "shepherds" (NIV, rōʿîm) may refer to the future national leaders who will come to rule over Israel, as interpreted in Targum (prnmyn). The phrase, "after my own heart" (NIV, kĕlibî) indicates that these good shepherds, may be the future rulers, who are chosen by Yahweh himself, who will "lead" (NIV, rāʿāh) Israel with the "knowledge" (NIV, dēʿāh) and "understanding" (NIV, śekel). The word "understanding" (NIV, śekel) denotes insights, and thus it may indicate the future shepherds are with capacity of making insightful decisions. McKane (1986, 2:73) suggested that these shepherds are descendents of David, who are perceived as "guardians of the Torah," and the broad interpretation of "shepherds" may refer to a new leadership of wisdom and care. The vocabulary "knowledge and understanding" (dēʿāh wĕhaśkkēyl) compared with Targum, "wbhkmh bmrʿ," denote a new breed of "shepherds" who will lead the community of Yahweh to their future destiny. Prosperity of Israel lies in the quality of rulers; wise rulers will prosper the nation and build the people (McKane 1986, 2:73).

The context of Jeremiah is political in nature. For example, Jeremiah 2:8 provides such context by signifying the meaning of "shepherds" (rōʿîm) as "leaders" (NIV) (Bright 1965, 15). From this examination, the rebellious leaders/rulers destroy Israel, and the future rulers who are obedient to Yahweh will restore Israel. Therefore, the governors have the responsibility of shepherd in leading with wisdom, protecting the people from destruction, and feeding with good knowledge and insights.

Shepherds are metaphors of leaders in the positive, as well as negative sense. Jeremiah 6:3 describes the attacks of shepherds (leaders/rulers) and their flocks (people) to the children of Benjamin. Possibly, these shepherds are rulers of foreign lands (see Bright 1965, 48). They lead the troops to eradicate all goods from Jerusalem. Agreed with McKane (1986, 141), the Hebrew here is "each man pastured with their hand" (rāʿû ʾîš ʾeyādô), may suggest a military commands for the divisional leaders for the eradication of the city.

Reider, though consent to Bright's view, he felt that the expression of each looking after his own pastures is vague. Rather, he agreed with Jouon that the "yād" may mean "bord" or "bordure", which can be translated as "secteur" (cited in McKane 1986, 141). This explanation fits the picture of Jeremiah 6:3 that each ruler, or shepherd, is a leader to his or her flock in the assigned group, under his or her pastoral care. Thus, leading activity is evident here.

Jeremiah 10:21 is an example of the metaphor of shepherd as rulers. In this verse, the foolish rulers are without discernment and wisdom because they do not consult Yahweh (McKane 1986, 231). These governors are pre-occupied with states matters that they do not allow Yahweh to participate in their political decisions by shunning out the prophets in the decision making process. Therefore, these foolish governors have no success in their ruling over their nations (McKane 1986, 231).

Leadership without discernment from Yahweh affects the political and social life of the community of Israel. Not only is the political stability of Israel affected, but the moral quality of the community of Israel (McKane 1986, 231). By the regulations of kingship in Deuteronomy 12:19-20 (NIV),

> Be careful not to neglect the Levites as long as you live in your land. When the LORD your God has enlarged your territory as he promised you, and you crave meat and say, "I would like some meat," then you may eat as much of it as you want.

From these verses, we see that the rulers of Israel are covenant keepers, and to lead Israel to be faithful to Yahweh. They fear Yahweh and obey his instructions. They are humble and do what is right. As shepherd, they are to exhibit the life of obedience to Yahweh. In so doing, they may succeed in governing.

The failure of good leadership in Israel explains the existence of its social dysfunction, moral deterioration, and national destruction. The national leaders, shepherds, did not care for the flock, the people of the nation, and the instructions of Yahweh were not properly imparted to strengthen the morality of the people. All these show that the condition of Israel when lack of good leadership is shove to the climax at exile and dispersion from their own land (McKane 1986, 231–232). The society of ancient Israel is very much regulated by the religious traditions that influenced their culture, morality, and social systems. Yahwism is at the center of the national and social life of the people of ancient Israel, and every aspect of their life relate to who they are in relation to Yahweh, their God. All these relationships tie onto the designated leader/ruler of Israelites nation that should direct the people closer to their God, through observing the covenant. In so doing, Yahweh will bless them. Therefore, shepherds/leaders/rulers are the ones who lead their flocks to observe their religious traditions, so that they have stability in society, moral living, and national prosperity and peace.

Jeremiah 12:10 illustrates the image of shepherd used in the prophetic literature of Jeremiah. The "shepherds" in the context of Jeremiah 12 may refer to the rulers of foreign invaders. The word "vineyard" (NIV, kerem) symbolizes Yahweh's land, and the invasion of the vineyard in Jeremiah 12:10 pictures the land of Canaan is devastated by the intrusion of foreign army. The total destruction of the land signifies the leading power of the shepherds or rulers, and that expresses the shepherd image of leading.

The image of shepherd in the prophetic literature of Jeremiah is one of rulers and of prophets. As a prophet, Jeremiah is a shepherd to Israel. Jeremiah 17:16 describes the defense of the prophet's office that he did not neglect his prophetic duties. He was a responsible shepherd to Yahweh's people, the sheep. This also speaks of Jeremiah as an assigned shepherd, and the sheep belong to Yahweh. He, Jeremiah, must also follow Yahweh's instructions. In the context of Jeremiah 17, Jeremiah defended that he has not tottered in obedience (McKane 1986, 410). It is evidential that the image of shepherd is an important figure to the political and spiritual aspects of the national life of Israel. Jeremiah 17:16 indicates the shepherding image of leading, though in moral matters.

Jeremiah 22:22 is another example of the critical role of shepherd. Targum, in agreement with the Masoretic Text, infers the shepherds "shall be scattered to every wind" (McKane 1986, 535). Duhm also consented that the Masoretic Text shall be preserved (cited in McKane 1986, 536). But if Masoretic Text shall remain as it is, the verse shall read as the shepherds shall be shepherded by the wind, which is the destructive power that chase them away because of disobedience (see McKane 1986, 536). Bright (1965, 142) suggested the driving away effect in the wordplay of "shepherds" and "lovers." However, the fact is that the word "shepherd" is the driving force in the form of wind destructively scattered the shepherds of the flocks. The consequence is shame and dismay come upon the residents of Lebanon (Jer 22:23). The destruction of shepherds, rulers, is the key to the destruction of a nation. Jeremiah 22:22 shows us that when rulers are slaughtered, disaster will come upon the people. Therefore, the shepherd image of protecting is critical and is evident.

Jeremiah 23:1–4 explicates a more vivid picture of irresponsible rulers, or shepherds, who affect the life of the people under their pastoral care. It is difficult to infer these shepherds to the rulers of Israel within the text of Jeremiah 23:1–4 (McKane 1986, 553). However, McKane suggested that the suffixes and verbs are in second person, indicates that the "ʿal" is equated with "ʾel". Thus, those condemned shepherds in verse 1 are the shepherds in verse 2 (McKane 1986, 553–554). But we have not identified the shepherds; are they foreign rulers, or Judean rulers.

The proposition of McKane (1986), though sound logical, is literary incompatible. The Hebrew here is "the sheep of my pasture" (ʾetṣōʾn marʿîtî) suggests no distinction from the "upon the shepherds shepherded my people" (ʿalhārōʿîm harōʿîm ʾetʿammî). The former is a general address to the rulers of a nation, and the latter is specifically refers to the rulers of Israel (see Bright 1965, 143). Jeremiah 22:18 (NIV) stated explicitly that the prophecy is address to "Jehoiakim son of Josiah king of Judah." With the flow of the context from Jeremiah 22:24–30, it supports the idea that it was the rulers of Israel mentioned in Jeremiah 23:1–4. The author transits the general condemnation of shepherds in verse 1, to the specific condemnation of the Judean rulers in verse 2 (contra McKane 1986). Thus, the shepherds in Jeremiah 23:1 and 2 are the Judean kings.

The condemnation is caused by the irresponsibility of the shepherds who ruled over the people. Bright (1965, 143) indicated that the verb "tend" (NIV, pāqad) in verse 2 first occurs with a sense of caring, and then occurs with a sense of calling for accountability. This is particularly in verse 2 where the rulers of Israel failed to care or attend to the welfare of the people. The result is dispersion from their homeland (see McKane 1986, 554).

Solution to this situation is that Yahweh will send another shepherd, who is responsible and perform according to his mandates. Jeremiah 23:4 (NIV), "I will place shepherds over them who will tend them, and they will no longer be afraid or terrified, nor will any be missing," also reflects the shepherd-sheep imagery in a relational manner (see McKane 1986, 557). This is an expression of shepherd image of leading and protecting that which is lacking in Israel may result in national destruction and desolation of security.

The descriptions of national rulers using the image of shepherd are common in the prophetic literature of Jeremiah. The text of Jeremiah 25:34 (NIV) infers that the rulers of the surrounding nations as "shepherds" and "leaders of the flock" (see McKane 1986, 651; Bright 1965, 162). In fact, the word "Leaders" is "majestic" ('addîr). Emphasis would be placed on the phrase "majestic of the flock" ('addîrēy haṣō'n), and that being a shepherd is in a prestige status, so people under his/her leadership care are honored. It is not simply as leader of the flock, as McKane understood. A shepherd is the majestic glory of the sheep. With the understanding of this prestige status of shepherds, it matches the inference of rulers or kings of a nation, including the inference to the kings of Israel, and more so to Yahweh.

The context of Jeremiah 25:34–36 tells us that the mighty rulers of the nations are unable to retaliate but to succumb to Yahweh's judgmental power. These ruler are powerful military commanders who can order the launch for war, yet they are as brittle as potteries when encounter the almighty God (McKane 1986, 652). When Yahweh's judgments come upon them, they shall disperse and be broken. The end of the verse describes the vulnerability of the mighty rulers when encounter the powerful God of Israel, "Hear the cry of the shepherds, the wailing of the leaders of the flock" (Jer 25:36 NIV).

In Jeremiah 25:34–36, it reflects a relationship between Yahweh and the shepherd. Although the metaphor of shepherd is used of deities, there is a difference when in used of Yahweh. Yahweh, as a shepherd, is mightier among other shepherds. This includes shepherds of Israel and of other nations. It is evident primarily in prophetic literature, and also in the literature of the Hebrew Bible. Thus, the image of shepherd in protecting is expressed in Yahweh's judgment on the rulers of the nations, so that Israel will be restored.

We have seen many examples of shepherd metaphor in the rulers of Israel and other nations, but Yahweh proves himself a responsible shepherd over Israel, his sheep. The text of Jeremiah 31:10 tells us that Yahweh as shepherd has the power to scatter his people and to gather them to himself. In the context of Jeremiah 31:1 (NIV), Yahweh promised that, "I will be the God of all the clans of Israel, and they will be my people." The significance of verse 10 is not simply the notion of Yahweh will gather Israel back, rather he will shepherd them like his flock (kĕrō'eh 'edrô). Yahweh, he will provide for the needs of his flock (see McKane 1986, 793). Thus, the picture here exhibits the image of shepherd in feeding and providing. The image of shepherd in providing for the needs of the flock is further expressed in Jeremiah 33:12. Yahweh promised to restore Israel and to provide them a place to rest; "there will again be pastures for shepherds to rest their flocks" (Jer 33:12 NIV).

Back to the image of foreign rulers in the expression of shepherd, Jeremiah 43:12 describes the devastation incur on Egypt by the invasion of the Babylonians. According to Rashi, the expression, "As a shepherd wraps his garment around him, so will he wrap Egypt around himself and depart from there unscathed," spells out how Nebuchadrezzar will deal with the spoils of Egypt. He will "wrap" (ma'áteh) the "land" ('ereṣ), may indicate a total destruction of Egypt, or grasp all things that are in that land.

The metaphorical image of "wrap" all things can be interpreted with two meanings, as suggested by McKane (1986). First, it may mean that the shepherd has a double-sided garment that accommodated to the changes of weather (McKane 1986, 1059). With this garment, all plunders shall be covered. Second, it can also mean that the Nebuchadrezzar purified the land of Egypt just as the shepherd purifies his garment through fire, indicated in Jeremiah 43:13 (McKane, 1060).

William L. Holladay (1989, 302) supported the idea of "wrap" up all things in the land of Egypt as wrapping up all plunders. Comparing with the idea of Nebuchadrezzar purifying the land of Egypt, which is the second suggestion of McKane (1986), Holladay is more impressed with the "wrap" simile of the first. The burning with fire in the text of Jeremiah 43:13 refers to the destruction of the temples of the gods of Egypt, which is a normal procedure for victory. The god, or gods of the defeated land, which is also the power of the people, shall be burned for destruction as the sign of victory over the deities of the enemies. To say that it is purifying the land may have spiritualized the simile; the simile of victory is preferred here.

Although the picture in Jeremiah 43:12 is one that the enemy carries away the possession of the defeated, it does reflect the posture how a shepherd carries his claimed possessions. Sheep are considered the possessions of shepherd, and the shepherd will wrap everything of his on his shoulders to bring them back. It is a depiction of leading the direction, and protecting by carrying on the shoulder. This is the metaphor of shepherd in leading and protecting his flocks, his possessions, to their folds.

Jeremiah 49:19 further describes the image of shepherd as rulers, but this time infer to Yahweh. Holladay (1989, 377–378) stated that the term "pasture" (nāweh) refers to "dwelling" in a poetic manner, just as "sucklings" ('ûlîm) refers to animals as well as "human infants," and "rams" ('ēylîm) may mean the "leaders of their people." Also, the word "pastureland" (nāweh) translated in NIV has the similar meaning as "dwelling." The context of Jeremiah 49 apparently concerns the reaction of Yahweh to his enemies. He appoints leaders as he desires because he is the shepherd, "what shepherd can stand against me?" (Jer 49:19 NIV). This affirms the status of Yahweh as a mightier shepherd than other shepherds, and he has the power to assign other shepherds to pasture the flocks (see Jer 25:34–36).

Jeremiah 50:6 is another example of irresponsible shepherds scattering the sheep. McKane (1986, 1256) commented that the sheep were lost because of enormous traveling activities without recollecting where they could rest and find safety. Duhm, however, advocated that the cause is the negligence of the shepherds. From Targum, it reads as if their trusted rulers to rebel against Yahweh misled Israel (McKane 1986, 1256). To this, some added that the "mountains" might imply to the high places where cultic activities took place (see McKane 1986, 1256). One of those advocates is Holladay (1989, 416), suggested that it is possible for the "mountains" to be a place of "fertility and worship."

From the context of Jeremiah 50, the picture of Yahweh gathering his people Israel, and that he urging them to come back to their folds. The shepherds have misled the people to the right pathway. This is supported by the Hebrew here, "their shepherds have led them astray," that states the culprit of the peoples' lost of destination is none other than their rulers. Therefore, it is an explicit example of the leading activity of the shepherd metaphor that can affect the well-being of the nation.

The metaphor of shepherd is positive when it is used of Yahweh. Jeremiah 50:19, spells out that Yahweh, as a shepherd, will restore Israel to their pasture. The word "dwelling" (nāweh) speaks of a place where the sheep call home. It is a place where they feed (rā'āh) on the pasture and "will be satisfied" (tīśbba'). In the shepherd care of Yahweh, he will lead them into his fold as his flock, feed them with good and nutritious pasture, and provide a safe place to live in peace; "with you I shatter shepherd and flock, with you I shatter farmer and oxen, with you I shatter governors and officials" (Jer 51:23 NIV). This spells out that Yahweh is the great shepherd because he exhibits the image of shepherd in leading, protecting, and feeding his people.

To summarize, the prophetic literature of Jeremiah portrays the metaphor of shepherd positively in Yahweh and negatively in the rulers of the nations, including Israel. Thus, it is advocating that Yahweh is a mightier shepherd among all shepherds, not only in power, but also in character. He is the shepherd who exhibits the metaphor of shepherd in the activities of leading, protecting, and feeding, and the flock shall follow their shepherd.

We have now observed the shepherd metaphor in the literature of Jeremiah. The literature of Lamentations does not contain the metaphor of shepherd, and therefore this study skip over to Ezekiel. To this, we shall now turn to the prophetic literature of Ezekiel.

Ezekiel

The metaphor of shepherd in the prophetic literature of Ezekiel is expressed in chapter 34. This chapter constitutes a significant understanding of the image of shepherd, particularly in reference to Yahweh. Like Jeremiah, Ezekiel 34 portrays Yahweh as the shepherd who will gather his sheep into their folds. In addition, this chapter spells out the judgment on the irresponsible shepherds who fail in their duties toward their sheep.

Ezekiel 34:2 (NIV) opens with the command to "prophesy against the shepherds of Israel." These shepherds are understood to be the rulers and kings of Israel, as in Eastern and Western ancient literature (Cooke 1936, 373). Cooke stated that the prophecy is wrapped in allegorical form to suggest that the subsequent prophecies are also similar. But allegory is a literary type that embraces ambiguity, and I would render it as simile. This is more palatable in the text where the biblical author describes by using the literary skill of simile to infer the actions of the irresponsible shepherds.

This chapter begins with the judgment on the shepherds who are selfish. The phrase "take care" (NIV, rāʿāh) indicates that the responsibility of the shepherds is to take care of the physical needs of the sheep, as described in verse 3 (NIV), "You eat the curds, clothe yourselves with the wool and slaughter the choice animals, but you do not take care of the flock." This simile expresses the negligence of those shepherds of Israel toward their sheep. They "eat" (ʾākal), "dress" (lābēš), and "sacrifice" (zābaḥ). Fat may imply the best, which is to be burned to Yahweh (see Lev 3). Cooke (1936, 374) indicated that,

> Animals slain for food used to be presented at the altar, so that all eating of flesh had something of a religious character. In the course of time, it became no longer possible to identify slaughter with sacrifice, as appears from Dt. 12:20–28, where a modification of the primitive custom is sanctioned; and the word for *sacrifice* could be used simply for *slaughter*.

If that is so, we should read verse 3 as the shepherds who have fed themselves with the best food and dressed themselves with the best clothing, yet did not attend to the sheep with the similar needs.

The devastation of the sheep is described here in Ezekiel 34:4-5 continues from verse 3. The negligence of the shepherd of Israel stage for the lack of care and fall prey to danger. Emphasis is on the phrase, "there was no shepherd" (Eze 34:5 NIV, miblî rōʿeh). It indicates that the lack of shepherd guidance will "scatter" (pûṣ) the sheep. Also, the phrase, "they became food" (NIV, wattihyeynāh lěʾāklāh) indicates that they are easy prey when there is no protection from their shepherd.

The scattering of the sheep is vast and the effect is great. Ezekiel 34:6 spells out the spreading of the sheep "over all the mountains and on every high hill" (NIV, běkālhehārîm wěʿal kālgibʿāh rāmāh) and "over the whole earth" (NIV, wěʿal kālpěnēy hāʾāreṣ). The crucial point of discerning a good shepherd lies in the phrase, "and no one searched or looked for them" (NIV, wěʾēyn dôrēš wěʾēyn měbaqqēš).

The primary target audiences in the text of Ezekiel 34:6 are the kings of Judah who failed to fulfill their role as the shepherd. These accusations from Yahweh underlie the royal duties the shepherds should have over the well-being of the Yahwistic community and the national social stability of Israel (Allen 1990, 161). Oppression of the poor by the strong is prohibited and the kings must execute justice in their judgment (see Dt 17:20). But justice is perverted and the people are disillusioned. The royal function should provide guidance to the people, but it is not available.

The term "search" (NIV, dôrēš) in Ezekiel 34:6 introduce the sense of "look out," and may probably fit into the scenario of searching the missing sheep (Allen 1990, 161–162). This is the intense emotional response from Yahweh when his people suffered under his appointed kings, who should oversee their welfare. Here, the image of shepherd is expressed in terms of protecting the sheep or people from harm, and to lead them to the right path as according to the desires of the great shepherd, Yahweh.

Ezekiel 34:7–8 continues the accusations of the shepherds due to their irresponsibility. Specifically, the proclamation is from Yahweh, "As surely as I live, declares the Sovereign Lord" (NIV, hay'ānî). The metaphorical shepherd is the kings of Israel in the context of Ezekiel 34. These verses have depicted the selfishness and irresponsibility of the Israel rulers over the people. They were set up as kings over the people of Israel by Yahweh, and should follow the precepts in Deuteronomy 17:18–20 (see Cooke 1936, 374). The sheep belonged to Yahweh ("my flock", NIV, ṣō'nî), and the kings were responsible to him. Septuagint, Coptic version, and Peshitta have the word "shepherds" (οἱ ποιμένεσ), but this is a weaker reading. Some suggested a total eradication of this verse, but Masoretic Text might be original and thus, retain the reading in the manuscript (see Cooke 1936, 374).

It is evident that verse 8 is the emotional reaction of Yahweh toward his shepherds. In the context of verses 5–6, the sheep were lost and needed guidance. This situation was reiterated in verse 8. The shepherds were self-centered to attend to the needs of the sheep, and failed to lead them to safety. The result is that the sheep "has been plundered" (NIV, lābaz wattihyeynāh) and "become food" (NIV, lĕ'āklāh). The shepherds failed in their responsibility to lead the sheep by gathering them back, but "did not search for my flock" (Eze 34:8 NIV, mē'ēyn rō'eh wĕlō'dārŝû). Yahweh responded to these shepherds with an "emotional vehemence," as indicated in the change of Hebrew construction (Allen 1990, 162). It is expressed in the reiteration of the term, "my flock" (ṣō'nî). Therefore, we see that the image of shepherd is expressed in leading the sheep out of danger, and lead them to the pasture or "sheepfold" where they will be fed.

With the emotional sentiment toward his sheep, Yahweh retrieved his sheep from his appointed shepherds' hands. Ezekiel 34:9 repeats the emphatic statement to the failing shepherds. In verse 10, "This is what the Sovereign LORD says" (kōh'āmar 'ădōnāy yĕhwih) indicates the source of authority that this proclamation based upon, which is Yahweh. Now from the hands of the shepherds ("from his hands", mîyādām), Yahweh will rescue his sheep into his folds. This action prevents further harm done to the sheep by the irresponsible shepherds ("I will remove them from tending the flock" NIV, wĕhiŝĕbbattîm mērĕ'ôt ṣō'n). The negative effect of their shepherding is indicated in the phrase, "the shepherds . . . feed themselves" (NIV, wĕlō'îr'û . . . hārō'îm 'ōtām). The word "still" or "again" ('ōd) emphasizes that the selfish shepherds cannot repeat the same action when the sheep is under the shepherding care of Yahweh. Therefore, the action of Yahweh retrieving the flock from the irresponsible shepherds is to prevent further harm will again incur upon the sheep.

Allen (1990, 162) commented that the image of shepherds in verse 10, is one belong to wild animal. The phrase, "from their mouths" (NIV, mippîhem) supported the idea. The solution to such situation is to "deliver" (nṣl), the people from the power of the kings, then peace and safety shall come upon them and their society. Allen (1990, 162) puts it another way, removed the "monarchy," also shares the sentiment.

The above observations point to the proclamation that are "against" the shepherds (NIV, ʿel rōʿîm), indicates a judgment to them. In addition, the word "hold accountable" (NIV, dāraš) indicates to "seek out" (see Cooke 1936, 375). The *textus Graecus originalis* has "on" (ʿal), which has the same meaning as "to" (ʾel), thus the Masoretic Text shall be retained. The interpretive significance of this passage is the judgment of Yahweh against his appointed shepherds who failed to exercise shepherding care to the sheep. All these suggest that the role of the shepherd is shaped by the activities of leading to the right path, protecting from harm, and feeding for growth. This expresses the metaphor of shepherd.

The shepherding responsibility now turns to Yahweh. In Ezekiel 34:11, the Hebrew "ʾănî" ("I" NIV) indicates that the responsibility is now on Yahweh, not on any foolish shepherds (Cooke 1936, 375). This introduces a theocracy that emerged by the cause of the defective monarchical system (Cooke 1936, 375). The kings were culpable for the devastation of the society and kingdom of Israel. They were responsible for the sufferings the people went through. The effect is the destruction of the national life and the disillusionment of Yahweh's protection when lies filled in their rebellious minds (see Cooke 1936, 375).

The text of Ezekiel 34:11 indicates that Yahweh "will search" (NIV, wĕdāraštî) for his people. Allen (1990, 162) stated that Yahweh determined to look after his people. He (1990, 162) also suggested that this might refer as the "Day of Yahweh," and that it would take the form of shepherding the flock, rather than judgment (see Eze 13:5; 30:3; Zep 1:5). The emphasis is given in the word "look after them" (NIV, ûbiqqartîm), which literally means attend to them. This denotes a sense of caring and attending to their needs. Here, we see that Yahweh as the shepherd would search and attend to Israel, his sheep. This image is one who leads, protects, and feeds, that which is the metaphor of shepherd.

Ezekiel 34:12 further elaborates the shepherding of Yahweh. The Hebrew "their flock" (ʿedrô) and "in days in the midst of scattered sheep" (bĕyômhĕyôtô bĕtôkṣōʾnô niprāšôt), indicate that Yahweh would rescue his lost sheep by searching among the scattering ones. Follow by, is to "deliver" (nāṣal) the sheep "from all places" (mikālhammqômōt). With the metaphor of shepherd as rulers, in this case, it may imply that Yahweh would rescue his sheep from their captors such as Babylon, Assyria, and Egypt (see Cooke 1936, 375).

The word "scatter" (pûs) highlights the devastating condition of the people of Israel when they are scattered in the foreign lands. As a caring shepherd, Yahweh would promise himself, with "as" (kĕ), to rescue the sheep, his people from the hands of their captors, and from their devastation. Thus is an expression of the image of shepherd in the figure of protecting.

The picture of feeding in the image of shepherd is exhibited in Ezekiel 34:13–14. The phrase "gather them" (NIV, wĕqibbaṣtîm) elaborates the process, and the phrase "from the countries" (NIV, minhāʾărāṣôt) supports that Yahweh would rescue his sheep from all the lands (see Cooke 1936, 375).

The restoration of Israel under the shepherding leadership of Yahweh may be signified by the word "their ground" (ʾadmātām). The foolish shepherds dispersed the sheep to foreign lands, but the good shepherd gathered them to their home soil. The result is that the destitute sheep would now "feed" (rāʿāh) on their own mountains and their own pasture lands.

The good shepherd will not feed with anything, but with "good pasture" (bĕmirʿehṭôb) (Eze 34:14). As part of the meaning of restoration, Yahweh will bring rest to his sheep; "they will lie down in good grazing land" (NIV, tirbbaṣnāh bĕnāweh ṭôb). Nutrition will be attended to, as indicated in the phrase, "they will feed in rich pasture" (NIV, ûmirʿeh šāmēn tirʿeynāh). This may be a prophetic imagination, as well as the future of Israel in the hope of Yahweh's return for his kingdom (Cooke 1936, 375). This is affirmed by the declaration from Yahweh, "declares the Sovereign LORD" (Eze 34:15 NIV).

Ezekiel 34:15 is an example of the shepherd metaphor of Yahweh. The first person pronoun emphasizes that Yahweh, as shepherd would attend to his sheep personally. A comment made that, "he who is the watch for (the messianic) salvation, the Holy One, blessed be He, will make Him to lie down in the Garden of Eden, as it is said in Ez. 34:15" (cited in Cooke 1936, 375–376). The image of shepherd in to "feed" (rāʿāh) and provide rest ("lie down", rābaṣ) is evident here.

As a shepherd, Yahweh performs the pastoral duty to the sheep when the foolish shepherds fail. Again, in Ezekiel 34:16, the first person pronoun indicates the personal attention to the devastating situation of the sheep. Yahweh will lead the lost (ʾābad) and scattered (nādaḥ) to return to his fold. He will provide safety by "bind up" (NIV, ḥābaš) the broken (šābār), and strengthen (NIV, ḥāzaq) the weak (NIV, ḥālāh).

The aspect of protecting the sheep is shown in the rest of Ezekiel 34:16. Yahweh will destroy (NIV, šāmad) the strong and fat oppressors. The word "shepherd" (NIV, rāʿāh) may imply retribution on the oppressors of Yahweh's sheep. Some suggest the reading "will keep," from Septuagint, Coptic versions, Peshitta, and Vulgate version, but the reading from the Masoretic Text is more appropriate to the context of punishing the oppressors. Also, the word justice (NIV, mišfāṭ) supports the idea of retribution (see Cooke 1936, 376).

The picture describes here may remind us of the "Day of Yahweh," where Yahweh will sort out the chaos created by the foolish shepherds. What is significant in this depiction is that Yahweh himself will tend the flock (see Allen 1990, 162). Allen pointed out that the word rāʿāh, "tend, feed" are used three times with reference to Yahweh in Ezekiel 34:11–16. This image of feeding by the good shepherd implies blessings come upon the sheep (Allen 1990, 162). As a shepherd, Yahweh is the ruler of Israel and will execute justice against the ene mies as a "royal virtue" (Allen 1990, 162). Thus, we see that these actions involved leading to safety, feeding with nutrition, and protecting by providing a safety ground, are facets of the shepherd metaphor. In this case, the image of shepherd in leading, protecting, and feeding are exhibited in Yahweh's model of shepherding, which could and have been exhibited in those appointed shepherds.

The development of Ezekiel has a twist after verse 16. The focus is now on the flock, no longer the shepherds (Eze 34:17). The phrase, "As for you, my flock" (NIV, wĕ'attēnāh ṣō'nî) set the focus differently. Previously, the foolish shepherds are judged with Yahweh's justice. Now, the justice rebounds to the flock's behaviors (see Allen 1990, 162). Allen (1990, 162–163) suggested that the context of Ezekiel 34:17–22 depicts the differentiation of leaders and followers, and the distancing of national leaders to his people. But the term, "my flock" (NIV, ṣō'nî) implies that the national leaders and people of Israel were under the jurisdiction of the great shepherd, Yahweh. The phrase, "between one sheep and another" (NIV, bēyn–śeh lāśeh) and between "rams and goats" (NIV, lā'ēylîm wēlā'attūdîm) may be a Hebrew idiom of differentiating the good and bad among the flock (contra Allen 1990).

What we see here is the justice (mišfāṭ) Yahweh executed on the appointed failing shepherds is now on the sheep. The wrongdoings of the sheep resemble that of those foolish shepherds. The terms, "trample" (NIV, rāmas) and "muddy" (NIV, rāfas) reflect the indifference of those sheep to others who were in need, just as those foolish shepherds has done, and thus will be judged similarly (see Cooke 1936, 376).

The significance of this verse 18 is that Yahweh, as a shepherd he has the duty to lead the sheep in justice. The shepherd's responsibility is not simply providing food, a place to rest, and delivering the sheep whenever they are in danger. It is critical to lead the sheep in justice. The lack of justice will result in moral deterioration and the well-being of the community will be at stake (see Cooke 1936, 377). Those appointed shepherds had failed to fulfill this task of building the Yahwistic community to flourish in characters that are pleasing to Yahweh. Therefore, Yahweh in restoring his flock will ensure that peace will be established, and justice will be exercised, so that the community of Israel may grow healthily and be strong. In so doing, the image of shepherd in leading is exhibited in Yahweh, and it is with justice.

The way to build the flock is to appoint a shepherd who dutifully performs the role of a shepherd. Yahweh will "will place over" (NIV, qûm) "one shepherd" (NIV, rō'eh 'eḥād) who is "David" (NIV, dāwid) (Eze 34:23). Cooke (1936, 377) stated that this "one shepherd," may refer to "the seed of David," and that may imply the restoration of the united monarchy. This reading seems logical because David was dead and his return was not literal. There is no contradiction between verses 15 and 23 because the latter is the installation of kingship after the restoration, while the former is the resolution to the chaotic situation (see Cooke 1936, 377). If this is correct, then literal seed of David may not be that shepherd, perhaps a description of an ideal shepherd that resembles

David (see Cooke 1936, 377). This ideal shepherd will perform the role of shepherd, as indicated with the repetition of the basic shepherding verb, "feed, tend" (rā'āh), to emphasize the task.

Allen (1990, 163) suggested that the appointment of the future "David," may imply the building of "Davidic monarch," and the returns of the theocracy, which is supported by the Hebrew "my servant" (NIV, 'abddî). In so doing, justice can be ensured as one who resembles David, a man after Yahweh's heart, sits on the throne. The covenant relationship will be restored as in pre-exilic era (see Allen 1990, 163). Allen (1990, 193–194) also emphasized that the role of this future king is to safeguard "a one-sidedly" politics. Thus, the restored flock of Yahweh will have a shepherd under Yahweh the great shepherd, in a covenant relationship, to fulfill the task of shepherding according to Yahweh's desires (see Isa 44:28).

Allen (1990, 194) stated that the new monarchical context will bring the "deuteronomistic conception" exemplified in Davidic rule, "as model and monitor of the covenant law" (see 1 Ki 3:6, 14; 9:4; 18:6; 23;3, 24–25). This relates to Ezekiel 37:24, where the Davidic monarch will safeguard the "moral and religion of his people" (Cooke 1936, 402). In Ezekiel 37:24, the description is vivid to relate shepherd to king, and lead the people to observe the covenant as in pre-exile monarchy (see Cooke 1936, 403). We must also take reference from the concept of kingship in Deuteronomy 17:14–20. There are many criteria concerning kingship. In relation to our discussion, the king "must be from among your own brothers," which fits the description of the Davidic monarch (Dt 17:15 NIV). In addition, the king is required to be conversant with the Law (Dt 17:18 NIV), and to lead the people with the Law of Yahweh, so that they may not deviate from the precept of Yahweh (Dt 17:19–20a). The result is an everlasting kingship to the king and "his descendants" in the land of Israel (Dt 17:20b). The deuteronomic conception of kingship supports the futuristic Davidic monarch in the prophecy of Ezekiel 34:24. Therefore, the image of shepherd in leading, protecting, and feeding will consummate in the future shepherd/king of Israel, who is chosen by Yahweh himself.

From these observations, the author of Ezekiel vividly describing the shepherding care of Yahweh to his people, his sheep, by leading them to their homeland, feeding them with good food for growth, and providing them a safe place to rest. In so doing, the image of shepherd is expressed in the activities of leading, protecting through providing, and feeding, especially in Yahweh.

The shepherd image is not exhibited in the literature of Daniel, and thus we do not examine this narrative. Now that we have observed the shepherd image in the prophetic literature of Ezekiel, we shall turn to Hosea to observe the shepherd metaphor exhibited in his prophetic message.

Hosea

The text of Hosea has rare references pertaining to the word "tend, feed," that which comes from the basic shepherding verb rāʿāh. Hosea 4:16 may consider as the textual evidence of the shepherd image, and Yahweh is the subject. The context here is regarding unfaithfulness of Israel to Yahweh, and being disobedient to him. According to Macintosh (1997, 165), the word "now" (ʿattāh) reflects a concluding sentence. Ibn Ezra and Kimchi read the sentence with a condition, "Had you not become obdurate, God would have pastured you like a sheep?" (cited in Macintosh 1997, 165). If this is correct, it implies that to verse 16b is interrogative, though without the interrogative particle (see Macintosh 1997, 165). Wolff (1974, 91) added that the usual precative function of "now" (ʿattāh) and the lack of interrogative denote a negative response of Yahweh. Both reading suggest a negative response from Yahweh.

There is an alterative reading to Hosea 4:16, according to Macintosh. The result of Israel's rebellion caused Yahweh to feed them improperly as described in the way sheep and cow were fed (Macintosh 1997, 165). This reading does not sound logical, because the verb "tend, feed" (rāʿāh) and noun "roomy place" (merḥāb) indicate feeding in richness and blessings (see Macintosh 1997, 165). It does not align with the proposition of Macintosh, though the image in Hosea 4:16 is a negative one. The more plausible reading is that Yahweh leads the people of Israel to the "roomy place" to be abandoned (McComiskey 1982, 71).

The metaphor of lamb and cow may present an effect after the judgment of Yahweh. Stuart (1987, 85) stated that the used of lamb and cow may refer to the state of change in Israel. The Hebrew, "roomy place" (merḥāb) may refer to the underworld, and thus it refers to the spacious netherworld (Stuart 1987, 85; see Ps 49:15 [Masoretic Text]). If this is correct, then the sin of Israel is of human nature. The result is that Israel will be cow in the netherworld, and that Yahweh cannot feed them like lamb unless they are in green pasture. It expresses the state of helplessness, not on the part of Yahweh, but Israel in their own stubbornness. This proposition does not tally with the literal meaning of the word "roomy place" (merḥāb). The usual word for underworld in Hebrew is "šĕʾōl" (grave, hell) and is not the same meaning as merḥāb (roomy place), which is used in Hosea 4:16. It is most probable to read as a spacious place, and may be lonely place, as McComiskey (1992, 71) suggested.

The conjunction "for" (kĕ) emphasizes forcefully the situation will be exactly the way it prescribed. It draws the conclusive ending of Israel if they continued in rebellion. Wolff (1974, 91) stated that the rebellion of Israel is caused by the hardening of hearts that impeded their capability to follow instructions from Yahweh. This incapacity of obedience resulted in the implementation of discipline from Yahweh. This leads us to understand an aspect of shepherd image in Yahweh that he will recant his promissory care if the sheep refused his pathway of security (see Wolff 1974, 91).

The metaphor of shepherd in Yahweh in the prophetic literature of Hosea portrays him as a father. One of the vivid examples of Yahweh's fatherly love is found in Hosea 11:1–11. Bullock outlined that the historical past of Israel is embraced as background information to the prophetic message of Hosea (11:1). The nostalgic language reminds Israel of Yahweh's fatherly care in their growing years (11:3). As a father, Yahweh led Israel with love bound in an intimate relationship (11:4). Bullock (1986, 98) continued that, from the imagery used in Hosea, Yahweh is a "tender and gentle father," whose love is boundless, and this is the fatherhood of Yahweh to Israel. The fatherly love of Yahweh is expressed in practical terms. With love, Yahweh has called Israel out of Egypt (Hos 11:1; 12:13), spoken tenderly and cared for them in the wilderness (Hos 2:14; 13:5), and secured them in the land of Canaan (McComiskey 1992, 184).

In addition to the father-shepherd love of God, Tidball (1986) makes a comparison between divine fatherly love and human fatherly love. The human father has limited patience, while the divine father has unlimited patience. The latter may be infuriated at times but not exhausted in grace. He has been patience to the rebellion of Israel and prepared to rescue his people (Hos 11:9–11). This is an emblem of shepherd attitude. Indeed, the fatherhood is also a facet of the shepherd metaphor.

From the above, we see that Hosea 4:16 pictured a mood of judgment. Andersen and Freedman (1980, 377) contended that the word "to shepherd" does not align with the judgment of Yahweh, and that it should be read as "to rule." They prefer the traditional meaning of "to graze bare," in the context of judgment (Andersen and Freedman 1980, 377). This reading is not logical to the context of Hosea 4:16. By doing so, we constrain ourselves to the limitation of the concept of feeding when referring to the verb rāʿāh. This verb rāʿāh has broader dimensions when used in different context. It can mean lead, protect, and feed. The shepherd should feed the sheep with good pasture, but in Hosea 4:16, the responsibility was impeded by the rebellion of Israel, and because of this, they were improperly fed.

At the same time, the shepherd is to lead the sheep to the right path so that they will not be lost. Discipline may be implemented where necessary, to keep the sheep safe. Just as the ideal shepherd in Ezekiel 34:37, lead the sheep to do Yahweh's desires, so is Yahweh, in Hosea 4:16, lead them to the right path, but with a hostile action yet in the context of fatherly love in Hosea 11:1–11 (see McComiskey 1992, 184–195).

To summarize, the metaphor of shepherd in leading, protecting, and feeding is exhibited in Yahweh in the prophetic literature of Hosea. The shepherd metaphor includes discipline the obdurate sheep in the hope that they will return to the right path, and will not be lost. Guidance is a key element in shepherding responsibility to enable the sheep to return to the shepherd safely.

A new facet of shepherd is fatherhood, which is critical to the attitude in shepherding the sheep. The fatherly love motivates the shepherding process, and patience to oversee the progress of growth. This is the image of shepherd in a constructive meaning expressed in the figure of leading, feeding, and protecting. Now that we have observed the shepherd image in the prophetic literature of Hosea, we shall turn to Amos to continue our study of shepherd metaphor.

Amos

Like the text of Hosea, the text of Amos also rarely contains textual evidence pertaining to the image of shepherd. The scarcity of references does not mean to ignore this book for the study of shepherd metaphor. We should make the best out of the references to understand the shepherding image in the prophetic literature of Amos.

The picture of shepherd portrays in Amos 3:12 is the aspect of protecting. Similar to Hosea 4:16, the context of Amos 3:12 is the judgment against Israel by using the simile of severely injured people, in reference to Yahweh as "the shepherd" (hārōʿeh) (see Andersen and Freedman 1980, 408). One may read as though Yahweh is the lion, just as in Hosea 5:14 (NIV), "For I will be like a lion to Ephraim," but the phrase, "As a shepherd saves" (Am 3:12 NIV, kaʾăšer yaṣṣîyl) seems to infer rescuing Israel, rather than devouring them (Andersen and Freedman 1989, 408). Although the description is in a devastating state, it does draw us to the protecting activity of the shepherd metaphor (so Andersen and Freedman 1989). However, Niehaus (1992, 386) painted a different picture that the nation will perish under the attack of Assyrian army, and only a small portion of Israel will be spared. This is probably a more appropriate reading of the text.

The text should not be used to determine the failure or success of a shepherd. The context is that Yahweh will judge Israel through their enemies. Israel's persistent defiance of Yahweh's instructions would produce the result of decimating parts of body and material possessions. Yahweh, as usual, would send a shepherd to rescue, but the severity of damage resembled to one that bitten by a lion, severely injured and left with incomplete physical appearance. The later part of the verse indicates the material loss caused by the attack; "so will the Israelites be saved, those who sit in Samaria on the edge of their beds" (Am 3:12 NIV). Finley (1990, 191) suggested that this description depicts the death of the animal and futility of deliverance. However, the shepherd is required to rescue the flock despite it is too late.

Another discussion of the word "rescue" (nāṣal) can be seen in conjunction with the preposition "so" (kēn). Niehaus (1992, 386) stated that the juxtaposition of "so," prior to "rescue" may infer the sense of snatch away, rather than the usual sense of deliver or save. This is due to the severity of judgment that though the shepherd performed the rescue, it was too late to recover the full physical body of the sheep. The action of snatch denotes that the shepherd was fighting a losing battle, only managed to removing parts of the sheep from the devourer.

To summarize, the image of shepherd is expressed in protecting the flock to the best. However, the shepherd is not responsible for the consequence of the rebellious flock that refused to follow instructions. The shepherd is to lead, protect, and feed, and the flock is to follow. Thus far, we have observed the shep herd image in the prophetic literature of Amos; we shall now turn to Micah to observe the shepherd metaphor.

Micah

Textually, Micah contains the metaphor of shepherd in the latter part of the book. Particularly in chapter 5, the context of prophecy concerning Bethlehem brings the notion of a shepherd will rise among their own people.

The image of shepherd is expressed through Micah 5:3 [4 NIV] in full array. The shepherd shall "stand" (ʿāmad) denotes the posture of shepherding ("shepherd", rāʿāh), or the posture of a king (see Andersen and Freedman 2000, 469). What is significant here is that the "strength" (ʿōz) of the shepherd originates, not from himself, but from Yahweh (see Smith 1911, 105). This reminds us that the appointed under-shepherd, as in Ezekiel, must rely on the strength of the great shepherd, Yahweh. The following phrase, "in the glorious name of Yahweh his God" (bigʾôn šēm yĕhwāh ʾĕlōhāyv) imply the source of strength to where it belongs (Mic 5:3 [4 NIV]). Thus, the shepherd performs his duty with the strength and in the name of Yahweh.

By the power of the commission, the shepherd shall keep the flock in the land. The Hebrew here "live secure," suggests the implication of security under this coming shepherd. But the verb "dwell" (yāšab) does not carry meaning of safety (see Smith 1911, 105). Andersen and Freedman (2000, 469) suggested that the shepherd functions as a protector, just as a king protects his people. Waltke (1993, 707), however, argued that the particle kî ("because") justifies the case of dwelling in security. This is because the verb "stand" (ʿāmad) is used metaphorically in court setting in the culture of the ancient Near Eastern to denote an ideal kingship that takes care of his people. However, in the case of messiah, it denotes the reality of security that is to come. Waltke (1993, 707) explained that it may be an exploitation of Davidic tradition in the form "lead, defends, and cares," as a shepherd for his flock, used in Micah 5:1-5 and in Ezekiel 34:23–24. In addition, the phrase, "to the ends of the earth" (Mic 5:3 [4 NIV]) affirms that the security is in the hands of this coming shepherd.

The strength of Yahweh given to the shepherd and that, which they rely, may depend on the relationship between the shepherd and his God. The Hebrew here, "in the strength of Yahweh" (bĕʿōz yĕhwāh) and "in the glorious name of Yahweh his God" (bigʾôn šēm yĕhwāh ʾelōhāyv) support a personal relationship (Mic 5:3 [4 NIV]). Some support the reading of dwelling in safety, because the language of the Masoretic Text implies that the pastoral care of a capable leader will eradicate fear (Waltke 1993, 707).

The image of shepherd exhibited in the coming shepherd among Israel extends the dimension of shepherding in the strength and in the name of the great shepherd, Yahweh. We also see that the metaphor of shepherd in protecting, feeding, and leading the flock in the posture of "stand," "feed," and the implied "dwell in safety."

Micah 5:3 [4 NIV] describes the image of shepherd equivalent to rulers of Israel. The numbers of shepherd raised in the future are the numbers of rulers, and they would retaliate against their enemies, and in this case, against the Assyrians. Smith (1911, 108) explained that the two numbers have to do with the expression of indefiniteness. Therefore, Yahweh will raise indefinite shepherds or rulers to lead Israel against their enemies.

The phrase, "treads upon our soil" (Mic 5:4 [5 NIV], "he tread in our palaces," îdrōk) supports the royal connotation, and the shepherds raise to fight against the Assyrians are defenders of the throne. Strengthen by the term, "leaders of men" (NIV, "princes of man", nĕsîkēy) in the collocation of numbers, these shepherds are the rulers of Israel. Smith (1911, 108–109) is right to say that the demands of rulers will be made accordingly; "They will rule the land of Assyria with the sword, the land of Nimrod with drawn sword. He will deliver us from the Assyrian when he invades our land and marches into out border" (Mic 5:6 NIV).

A messianic reading of Micah 5:4 (NIV) comes from Waltke (1993, 709) that the designation of "shepherds" (rō'im) is identified with the future ruler, messiah. Although this is theologically verifiable in the New Testament, especially in Matthew 2:6, the context of Micah 5:4 does not justify the messianic figure. At best, it can be explained as the revolving thought of messianism at the early stage. What the context suggests is a military retorting force that comes from military leadership of the future. Agreed with Smith (1911, 109), the terms shepherds and rulers are designation of military rulers. Therefore, messianism, understood in New Testament theology, is prominent in the New Testament perspective, but is foreign in the Hebrew Bible; at least at this point.

The ending of the prophetic literature of Micah casts the shepherd image once again on Yahweh that he will "shepherd" his "people" ('am) (Mic 7:14) (Smith 1911, 153). Waltke (1993, 758) stated that the term, "your people" ('ammāk) should read as an apposition, with the "flock" (ṣō'n) functions as an accusative. The term, "sheep" (ṣō'n) suggests that the people of Israel are sheep to Yahweh. The Hebrew here, "your possession" (naḥălāteāk) indicate the connection between the "shepherd" and "your people" ('ammāk) (see Smith 1911, 153; Waltke 1993, 758). These expressed the relationship between the shepherd and the sheep, just as Yahweh own the people of Israel and they belong to him.

The concept of shepherding keeps us focus on the leading, protecting, and feeding aspects of the metaphor. The phrase, "lives by itself in a forest" (Mic 7:14 NIV, šōknî lĕbādad ya'ar) suggest a manner of dwelling free from danger (Waltke 1993, 758; see Deut 33:28; Ps 4:9 [8 NIV]; Jer 49:31). This is because the word rā'āh in verse 14b is jussive, and in verse 14a, is imperative. Waltke (1993, 759) argued that the verb, "shepherd" (rā'āh), that is transitive is used as intransitive, and that it means "to graze, feed." Therefore, the shepherd is to lead the sheep to feed on the land of Bashan and Gilead.

Micah 7:14 suggests a picture of restoration of the monarchy of Israel as in the pre-exilic era. Smith (1911, 153–154) stated that the prophet urges a restoration of the pre-fall glory of Israel, and the territories that are long lost, even to the east of Jordan. The phrase, "feed in Bashan and Gilead" (NIV, îr'û bāšān wĕgil'ād), support the proposition of Smith. Moreover, the concept of restoration connects to the Hebrew here, "as in the days of old/forever" (kîmēy 'ôlām), gives the idea of returning to the past. It is to read Micah 7:14 as Yahweh's delivery promise that he will lead the people of Israel to a place of safety, just as he had done in the past, and restore to them the glorious days of nation formation (Mic 7:15 NIV).

To summarize, the literature of Micah portrays the image of shepherd as rulers and refers to the future rulers and Yahweh himself. The picture consists of the activities of leading, protecting, and feeding of the metaphor of shepherd, and concludes in the model of shepherding exhibited in Yahweh. Now that we have observed the shepherd image in Micah, we shall now turn to Nahum to observe the image in its prophetic literature.

Nahum

The literature of Nahum is also rarely contains references pertaining to the imagery of shepherd. The concept may have implicitly infused with the text, and it is our purpose to observe the references of the imagery in the literature of Nahum.

The reference to the image of shepherd is in Nahum 3:18, and is the image of ruler or king. The term, "king" (melek) is used, and in relation to the term, "your shepherds" (rō'eyāk), indicates that both terms are equivalent. The term, "your shepherd," is addressed to the city, and suggested the idea that the rulers of Assyria are shepherds to the people at that time (Smith 1911, 353).

The importance of shepherds, or kings to the city is comparable to shepherds to the flocks. The Hebrew here, "slumber" (nûm), may be read as death (Na 3:18 NIV) (see Smith 1911, 353). This may imply that the city is without rulers. The people are left to themselves to defend the city, and as good as left to death. However, the second part of Nahum 3:18 suggest a more devastating situation. The people of Assyria who are without shepherds, or rulers to lead them, they abandoned the city and scattered over places ("your people are scattered upon the mountains and there is none to gather them," nāfōšû 'ammāk 'alheharîm wĕ'ēyn mĕqabbēṣ). This suggests that "slumber" in Nahum 3:18 can be read as "death."

The definite inefficiency of the Assyrian rulers is the key to the fall of the city. The sequential collocation of the terms, "asleep" (nûm) and "settle" (šākan) denote "a sleep of finality" (Pattern 1991, 111; see Ps 94:7; Isa 26:19). Therefore, this verse expresses the devastation of the city that is without leadership, and result in dispersion (Patterson 1991, 112). The city has no rulers, or shep herds to gather them to the fold; it is a state of devastation.

To summarize, the image of shepherd exhibits in the literature of Nahum pertaining to the activities of leading and protecting. Without leadership, the city is defenseless, and prone to disaster, in the case of Nahum, it is dispersion. Thus, the metaphor of shepherd is evident in the prophetic literature of Nahum. Now that we have observed the shepherd image in Nahum, we shall turn to Zechariah to observe the imagery in its literature.

Zechariah

The literature of Zechariah consist some significant texts for the study of the metaphor of shepherd. It contains references pertaining to the irresponsible shepherds, in particular.

The text of Zechariah 10:2 describes the misery of Israel without a shepherd and in need of one. It reflects the result of deviating from the instructions of Yahweh to follow other gods (Mitchell 1912, 287). The Hebrew here, "like sheep" (kĕmósō᾽n) describes precisely the condition of Israel, and "they pull out" (nāsʿû) describes the situation where they were lost and aimless (McComiskey 1998, 1177). The Hebrew here, "they will bend down" (yaʿănû) is im perfective and may imply an ongoing action (see McComiskey 1998, 1177). All these suggest that the perennial affliction of Israel is caused by the lack of a shepherd. The people, pulling out, were wandering like sheep without a shep herd to lead them. Situation will persist if no shepherd is designated to lead them. But the affliction was due to Israel's rebellion, on the part of the rulers, to Yahweh's instructions.

The text of Zechariah 10:3 continues to describe the situation of Israel. Mitchell (1912, 288) suggested that the Hebrew, "the shepherds" (hārōʿîm), refers to foreign rulers, since in verse 2, the nation of Israel has no shepherd. This expression indicates that shepherd is a metaphorical term for rulers (see McComiskey 1998, 1179).

These leaders or rulers translated from the Hebrew, "he-goats" (ʿattûdim) who were sought out by Yahweh are "the shepherds" designated to lead the flock. The verb, "seek out" (pāqad) does not indicate any sense of punishment, and in the context, it may infer accountability of their leadership (so McCo miskey 1998). What that means is that Yahweh will call the shepherds for ac countability by their responsibilities, so they will be judged accordingly and appropriately (McComiskey 1998, 1179). Thus, the picture in Zechariah 10:3 is the judgment of the shepherds in the general sense, upon those shepherds who failed to lead their flock, and the result will be the replacement of rulers or shep herds. This exhibits the status of shepherds as rulers who are the leaders of so cial changes. It is this prominent activity of leading in the metaphor of shepherd that is expressed here.

The judgment of Yahweh to the foreign rulers continues in Zechariah 11:3. In this verse, the devastation of Israel's enemies is described by who was once mighty, is ripped off their power by Yahweh. Doubtlessly, the shepherds in Zechariah 11:3 are rulers of the foreign land, as indicated in verse 1 (see Mitchell 1912, 197).

The Hebrew pual, "splendid" ('addîr) of the enemies is to "be devastated" (šuddad), expresses the destination of the kingdom's glory is destruction. In the image of shepherd, the description is the destruction of the shepherd's pasture that he feeds the sheep (Mitchell 1912, 297). The description of the destruction of the enemies continues here. The Hebrew, "wailing of" (îllat) and "roaring of" (ša'ăgat), expressed the devastation of these foreign rulers. What they were proud of ("pride", gĕ'ôn) is now destroyed. They were powerless to restore their glory. This denotes the image of shepherd in leading and protecting, and that the shepherd is the key to success and failure.

The judgment against the foreign rulers in Zechariah 11:3 amplifies in Zechariah 11:4. The direct command of Yahweh is the authority of judgment; "Thus said the LORD my God" (Zec 11:4). Yahweh dispatches the shepherd to destruction the flock. The Hebrew here, "to shepherd" (rĕ'ēh), generally means, "to feed or shepherd," but sufficient references connote as "to tend or shepherd" (1 Sam 16:11; 17:15; 25:16; Jer 23:2) (McComiskey 1998, 1191). In this case, the general meaning of rĕ'ēh is applicable here, since it refers to the foreign rulers in the context of judgment (contra McComiskey 1998). The word, "slaughter" (hărēgāh), spells out the responsibility of the shepherd is to bring destruction to the flock. Here, I will not focus too much on the interpretative problems of the text. What must be highlighted is the term, "shepherds," which is used as a synonym for "kings," and in this context, a foreign king (see Mitchell 1912, 303). Thus, this expresses the image of shepherd in the activity of leading, but in this context is to destruction of the flock.

The literature of Zechariah casts the image of shepherd to Yahweh. In Zechariah 11:7, the solution to the doomed situation is the replacement with a new shepherd, who has "two staffs" (šĕnēy maqlôt). This could due to the culture of sheep traders who are ruthless in business, killing the sheep for the sake of business trade (Mitchell 1912, 204). By replacing the shepherd, the sheep will not encounter disaster under a trader. Yahweh is the replaced shepherd in Zechariah 11:7. The two staffs characterized the model of shepherding in Yahweh. Yahweh will shepherd the sheep himself, as supported by the phrase, "and I pastured the sheep" (wā'er'eh 'ethaṣṣō'n). The two staffs are symbolically shepherds of characteristics; it is with "Favor" and for "Union" (Zec 11:7 NIV) (Mitchell 1912, 305). With this, we may conclude that Yahweh shall rule the people with "kindness" (nō'am) and "union" (hōblîm), and the shepherding leadership must observe this responsibility (so Mitchell 1912).

The two staffs entail the responsibility of a shepherd. The first staff is "kindness," denotes that the shepherd must treat the sheep with kindness. The second staff is "union," denotes that apart from feeding and leading the sheep, the shepherd has the responsibility to disperse disharmony among the sheep. Mitchell (1912, 305) indicated that these meanings of the staffs may have been the thoughts in the prophet's mind when naming the staffs.

The two staffs represent the way Yahweh shepherd his sheep, but not in a restrictive sense. Mitchell (1912, 305) called these requirements "ideals" or "obligations." But we see that from Zechariah 11:9 onwards, Yahweh refused to be the shepherd. The breaking of the two staffs in Zechariah 11:10–14 indicates the breaking of "favor" and "bond" between the shepherd and the sheep, and between the deity and the nation (McComiskey 1998, 1194). In this context, he is not being irresponsible but simply responded appropriately to the chaotic situation. The persistent disobedience of the sheep requires shepherding discipline for correction. Thus, whatever it was, the image of shepherd exhibited here is the activity of leading in fostering unity and protecting with kindness to the sheep.

As implied above, though the shepherd has the responsibility to shepherd the sheep with kindness and to foster unity, it is not legalistic to fulfill. Zechariah 11:8 tells us that the unremorseful attitude of the sheep results in the shepherd's declining of fulfilling his role (see Mitchell 1912, 307). This is evident in the Hebrew, "be shortened" (qāṣar) and "become tired of" (bāḥălāh bî), that the shepherd is infuriated with the sheep (see McComiskey 1998, 1195). The result is destruction ("be destroyed", nikĕḥad) in totality (McComiskey 1998, 1194; see Ex 23:33; 1 Ki 13:34; 2 Ch 32:21; Ps 83:5 [4] NIV).

Yahweh is one who overseeing his sheep and determining the appropriate action to be taken. The shepherds assigned in Zechariah 11:4–5 in its contexts seem to refer to the foreign rulers. But the first person pronoun indicates that it is Yahweh himself who send the flock to destruction because of their religious infidelity. They violated the covenant relationship between the shepherd and the sheep. As a shepherd, Yahweh should shower kindness and foster unity, as all other shepherds, but more so, he incurred discipline on the sheep. This is, as mentioned earlier, for correction. Thus, it expresses the idea of leading in the righteous path within the metaphor of shepherd.

The attitude of Yahweh toward the rebellious sheep is harsh (Zec 11:9). The Hebrew here, "let it be destroyed" (hanikkḥedet) and "let . . . be consumed" (tōʾkalnāh) indicate the severity of Yahweh's anger. The Hebrew, "each other" (rĕʿûtāh) affirm the idea. Mitchell (1912, 307–308) read this as the indifference of the shepherd, and that probably comes from his reading that this shepherd is someone else, not Yahweh. However, this may be a misconception.

The highlight of this destruction is in verse 10, where the relationship is broken represented by the breaking of the two staffs. The two staffs symbolized the covenant relationship between the shepherd and the sheep (see Mitchell 1912, 308; McComiskey 1998, 1197). The Hebrew here, "cut off" (kāḥad) is used in the making of covenant, and it applies here. It induces the breaking of the staffs as the breaking of covenant, and therefore, Yahweh endorsed the an nulling of the covenant; "who were watching me, knew that it was the word of the LORD" (Zec 11:11 NIV).

The breaking of the second staff signifies the breaking of the harmonious relationship among the flock. In Zechariah 11:14, the Hebrew, "cut off" (kāḥad) express the severity of brotherhood between Israel and Judah. Therefore, Yahweh returns the rebellious sheep with fierce anger exhibited in the removal of kindness in the covenant, and the union between brotherhoods. This is shepherding discipline.

The severity of Yahweh's anger continues to flame on the sheep. This time, Yahweh commands the prophet to be the foolish shepherd. In the prophetic literature, the foolish shepherd is one who fails to see Yahweh's purposes and is helpless when they are fulfilled (Mitchell 1912, 315). In wisdom literature, the Hebrew, "foolish" ('ĕwîlî) has a moral construction and that is the lack of godly wisdom. Similarly, foolish shepherd in prophetic and wisdom literature depicts as one who does not understand the will of Yahweh and act foolishly. Therefore, the foolish shepherd may lead the sheep into disaster (McComiskey 1998, 1205).

The foolish shepherd, compared to the good shepherd, will destroy the well-being of the community, than build a resting place. Zechariah 11:16 describes the characteristics of a foolish shepherd. He does not "take care" (pāqad) of those who are "to be destroyed" (hannikḥādôt). He does not "seek" (bāfaš) the "youth" (naʿar) who are wandering to the wrong path. He does not "make healthy" (yĕrapēʾ) the "broken" (nišberet). He does not "clasped" (kûl) the strong that "stand" (nāṣab). He "eats" ('ākal) the "flesh" (bāśar) of the "fat, or new" (bĕrîʾ), that are cattle, as supported by the Hebrew here, "and their hoofs tearing off" (ûparsēyhen yĕpārēq). The characteristics of a foolish shepherd are evident here. His irresponsibility is marked by cruelty to the sheep under his care (Mitchell 1912, 315). The shepherd refused to seek the lost, and let the youth wandered off is denoted by the lack of the Hebrew, waw ("and") (see McComiskey 1998, 1205). The negative Hebrew, "not" (lōʾ) repeatedly appears three times in the verse signifying the shifting of responsibility on the part of the shepherd. This is an example of bad shepherd. However, we must read within the context of Yahweh's judgment and the mandate of the metaphor of shepherd in the Hebrew Bible. It is the judgment of Yahweh in sending the foolish shepherd to destroy the flock who disobedient to him.

The context of Zechariah 11 is the judgment of Yahweh against Israel and Judah for their rebellion and disobedience through their wicked shepherd leadership. The literature of Zechariah concludes the image of shepherd with the slaughtering of the foolish shepherd. The text indicates the shepherd as "worthless" ('ĕlîl). What follows in the verse 17 of Zechariah 11 is the punishment the foolish shepherd deserved. The "sword" (ḥereb) signifies war is against the shepherd or king. The Hebrew here is, "his arm" (zĕrôʿô) with "upon" ('al), that denote the striking effect on the arm of the shepherd. This also describes the destruction of the defenseless power of the shepherd (see Mitchell 1912, 316).

The striking of "his right eye" (ʿēyn yĕmînô) adds to the predicament to indicate the inability to defend himself (Mitchell 1912, 316). The end of the verse simply amplifies the consequence of the foolish shepherd that is against Yahweh (see McComiskey 1998, 1207).

This picture of "worthless" shepherd provides the metaphor of shepherd, a flip-side of the same expression. The shepherd should lead the sheep, but a worthless or foolish shepherd lacks the ability to lead and protect the sheep. The metaphor of shepherd in Zechariah must surround the activities of leading, protecting, and feeding the flock.

The next picture of shepherd in the literature of Zechariah is chapter 13:7. Yahweh calls "my shepherd" (rōʿî), though for judgment. The shepherd is considered as "fellow, comrade" (ʿāmît). This denotes that the earthly shepherd is fellow-workers with Yahweh to lead the sheep. A shepherd is perceived as a leader, indicated by the phrase, "strike the shepherd, that the sheep will be scattered" (Zec 13:7 NIV).

The state of a shepherd is elucidated in Zechariah 13:7. Yahweh, the divine shepherd, will work along with the earthly shepherd, and the latter is accountable to the former in his responsibility. The relationship between Yahweh and the shepherd is intimate, because though are co-workers, the shepherd belongs to the shepherding care of Yahweh. Metaphorically, the king, who is under the jurisdiction of Yahweh, is an earthly co-worker with him to lead and feed the people, who are his sheep. However, this status does not exempt the shepherd from Yahweh's judgment. If they fail in their duties and responsibility, the people suffered under their unfaithful and foolish leadership (Mitchell 1912, 317). At the same time, they will be judged by Yahweh for failing to exercise shepherding care to the sheep. This expresses the image of shepherd in relation to the blessing or curse of the flock. Yahweh, once again, portrays himself as the superior shepherd over his appointed shepherd, and exercises discipline over them when they fail in their shepherding responsibility.

To summarize, the prophetic literature of Zechariah portrays the image of shepherd in positive and negative pictures. There are good shepherds who are like Yahweh, leading the sheep to the right path, protecting them from harm or danger, and feeding them to grow. But there are bad shepherds who fail in their duties to lead, protect, and feed the flock. They lead the sheep in the way that benefit themselves. Of course, in this context, Yahweh exercises judgment against his foolish sheep through designating foolish shepherd to lead them to destruction.

In the context of the shepherd metaphor, these shepherds have violated the mandate given to them. It is in this context, that we should read the passages contained the image of the bad shepherds. However, we anchor our understanding on the responsibility of the shepherd in the metaphor. The leading, protecting, and feeding responsibility is at the core of the metaphor of shepherd in the Hebrew Bible.

To this regard, Tidball's concept of pastoral theology is employed appropri ately. He outlined that, the responsibility of a shepherd works within a convention that he is the one "to feed the sheep, protect them," and has the ability to provide good substance for health, as well as to integrate the sheep as a flock (Tidball 1986, 46). Justice and righteousness are the virtuous character a shepherd must possess and exercise in his/her responsibility (Tidball 1986, 46).

The quality of a good shepherd in the Hebrew Bible is one who lives by the word of God. In providing, protecting and feeding, the king, prophet, or priest exercises the judicial role with righteousness and wisdom of Yahweh. Therefore, the image of shepherd is one who exercises judicial responsibility in justice and with wisdom, and the source is Yahweh.

To conclude the matter, the shepherding metaphor begins with Yahweh himself in his historical activities with Israel. Through the formulation of the nation of Israel, Yahweh appointed priests, prophets, and kings to provide the shepherding ministry to his people. All these appointments were set to protect the people spiritually and politically, as well as to provide for their living needs, spiritual and physical. The metaphor of shepherd discussed in the prophetic literature found its place in the historical contexts of the Hebrew Bible.

This presents the study of shepherd metaphor in the later prophetic literature with the activities of leading, protecting, and feeding. We shall now observe the shepherd metaphor in the Writings of the Hebrew Bible. To this, we now turn.

CHAPTER SEVEN

THE METAPHOR OF SHEPHERD
IN THE WRITINGS

The image of shepherd in the Writings of the Hebrew Bible is descriptive rather than prescriptive. There are different types of literature in this category of the Hebrew Bible. For example, Psalms are songs of expression toward circumstances and to Yahweh. But they are also the expression of the psalmists' theological perspective in an unsystematic way. There is wisdom literature which contained ancient wise sayings and practical wisdom that expressed the result of the fear of Yahweh. Also, there is a love song that expressed the intrinsic relationship between humans which reflects the relationship between Yahweh and humans. Since the Psalms express the inner feelings of the psalmists, they contain emotions toward life and circumstances. In a deeper sense, it is theology. Let us now turn to the Psalms.

Psalms

The most prominent text describing the image of shepherd is Psalm 23. This psalm is commonly used as the basis for the New Testament concept of shepherd with reference to Jesus Christ and pastors of the New Testament churches. What exactly this psalm has to portray about the image of shepherd is essential to the understanding of Yahweh as shepherd in the Writings of the Hebrew Bible.

The subject of Psalm 23 is Yahweh as the shepherd of David. In Psalm 23:1, the Hebrew, "my shepherd" (rōʿî) indicates the relationship of the between David and Yahweh, in that he is under the shepherding care of Yahweh, and Yahweh is his shepherd. The result of Yahweh's shepherding is described in the Hebrew, "not I lack" (lōʾ ʾehsār) on the part of David. Shepherd, here, is used as a frequent biblical and ancient Near Eastern metaphor for royalty (Isa 40:11; Eze 34; Ps 80). The sheep under the care of Yahweh will find them needing nothing (Briggs and Briggs 1906, 208). This is the feeding activity of the metaphor of shepherd.

On Psalm 23:1, Allen Ross stated that there is a deeper meaning than its description. He explained that the shepherd image utilized by the psalmist is for recollecting the memories of blessed life through Yahweh (see Ps 28:9; 80:1). Ross (1985) also affirmed that the shepherd image is used of David as a king. Hence, it is used as in the culture of the ancient Near East to refer to kings and leadership as shepherd (Ross 1985, 811). In other words, God uses an image that his own people could understand and relate, because of the cultural settings at that time.

This brings an important insight regarding the rulership of God—theocracy. Since the metaphor of shepherd is embraced by the kingship in the ancient Near East, similarly, Yahweh is legitimately the king and shepherd of Israel. These two roles are intertwined. In this perspective, rulers or kings may be equated as leaders.

Regarding the concept of God as shepherd, Ross drew our attention to the theological connection of the metaphor of shepherd with Jesus as the shepherd. He elaborated that the prophecy concerning the coming shepherd identified as Jesus in the New Testament. The shepherd and Jesus are shepherd (see Isa 40:11; Jn 10:14). Jesus is also called the "good shepherd," "great Shepherd," and "Chief Shepherd" (Jn 10:14; Heb 13:20; 1 Pe 5:4 NIV) (Ross 1985, 811). Therefore, the shepherd metaphor is a significant image that begins from Yahweh through Moses, judges, priests, prophets, kings, and eventually to the New Testament shepherd figure in the person Jesus Christ.

The word, "shepherd" in Psalm 23:2 exhibits Yahweh's leadership to the sheep. He "guides" (nāhal) David, the sheep, to "let him lie down" (yarbbîṣēnî) in "new fresh green pasturage" (binʾôt dešeʾ). This denotes the shepherd leads the sheep, not in terms of military connotation as in most cases, but leads them to where the fresh food, so that they may feed themselves and grow. In the case of Psalm 23, this is a rare situation to shepherds, because the land of Palestine is not ideal to have green pasture except in rainy season (Briggs and Briggs 1906, 208).

The text of Psalm 23:2–3a exhibits another aspect of leading in the metaphor of shepherd. Yahweh, the shepherd, "guides" (nāhāl) David, his sheep, "upon" (ʿal) "waters of rest" (mēy mĕnuḥôt), so that David can "returning" (yĕsôbēb) his "soul" (nāfaš). This shows that the shepherd, not only feeds the sheep with green pasture, but also guides the sheep to a refreshing place where the sheep can regain his strength (see Briggs and Briggs 1906, 208). Compared to Psalm 49:15, "death" (māwet) is the shepherd of sheol (see Dahood 1966, 146). The Hebrew here, ʿal can mean "near" in the Ugaritic practice (Dahood 1966, 146). Therefore, it supports the proximity of the resting place, and that resuscitation is at hand. This expresses the leading activity of the shepherd metaphor in bringing life to the sheep.

The leadership of a shepherd is toward righteousness and justice. In Psalm 23:3b, Yahweh now "guides" (nāhāl) David to the right path; the Hebrew here is, "track" (maʿggāl) of "right" (ṣedeq). The word, "right" consists meaning of "justice" (Dt 1:16), and as an adjective, "just, righteous" (Dt 16:18). Dahood (1966, 146) inclined to stretch the sense of "lead" into paradisal meaning, but this has no support from the biblical text. In fact, the picture of earthly manifestation of Yahweh's truth seems more appropriate, as the verse ends with the reason of his action, "for his name's sake" (Ps 23:3b NIV).

In Psalm 23:2–3a, the image of providing food and water express the recovery process of the sheep's condition on the dutiful actions of the shepherd (Briggs and Briggs 1906, 209). Yahweh guides the sheep toward the destination of safety where the sheep can rest and restore his soul. This guidance is a direction to blessings and not simply to destination (Briggs and Briggs 1906, 209). Here we see that the guidance of a shepherd involves character and spiritual aspects of growth. Briggs and Briggs (1906, 209) added that the name of Yahweh, as a shepherd, "is involved in guiding rightly." This is shepherding responsibility of leading.

The unwavering care of the shepherd continues in the description of Psalm 23:4. Here, the sheep "not fear evil" (lōʾîrāʾ rāʿ) because the shepherd "stand with me [him]" (ʿimmādî). This denotes a trust relationship between the shepherd and the sheep. The rest of verse 4 amplifies it. The defense from the rod, and support from the staff, made the timid sheep to be courageous to walk through "dark valley" (gayĕ ṣalmāwet) (Briggs and Briggs 1906, 210). Briggs and Briggs (1906, 210) added that the rod and staff are the assurance of safety, guidance, and direction to the destination where the sheep should go, in the sense that fear is removed, discomfort or worries is tranquilized and settled.

The shepherd continues his tender care to the sheep in hosting a banquet to assume the responsibility of protecting the sheep before the enemies (Ps 23:5). It is not a feast without hostility. The Hebrew, "hostile toward" (ṣārar) supports this idea. Briggs and Briggs (1906, 210) commented that the enemies are present but caused no danger.

The scenario of the banquet belongs to the custom of the orient. In that custom, the host honors the guests by putting oil on their heads (Briggs and Briggs 1906, 210). This is prior to the guests entering to the banquet (see Am 6:6). Lane added that in the modern custom, the host will sprinkle perfume on the guest (cited in Briggs and Briggs 1906, 210). Briggs and Briggs (1906, 210) read this verse as a royal entertainment to special guests. The quality and quantity of food and wines are excellent, especially the wine that makes the heart glad. Some suggested that it may resemble the Eucharist of the early church, but that may have extended its meaning beyond the context of Psalm 23.

What we see here in Psalm 23:5 is a feast that the sheep is fed in the presence of hostility, but yet without fear, just as walking "through the valley of the shadow of death, I will fear no evil" (NIV). The word translated "anoint" (NIV, "be made fat, be revived," dāšēn) has a sense of making the one who comes to be pleasant. This has no special power as the usual connotation of the word "anoint" used in Christian church. What it implies is that the host is responsible to oversee the well-being of the guests. This includes safety and peace. The sheep in the banquet, though faced with hostility, he is safeguarded by the presence of the shepherd. Thus, the protecting activity of the metaphor of shepherd is exhibited here.

The Psalm 23 ends with an assuring note from the shepherd to the sheep. The emphatic "surely" ('ak) in Psalm 23:6, affirms the certainty of the following blessings in "goodness" and "faithfulness" (tôb wāhesed). The interesting picture in this clause is the pursuing of the sheep by the two promises, as indicated in the word, "pursue" (rādap). The New International Version translation of the Hebrew, "follow," has reduced the intensity of the action.

The next highlight is the dwelling in the house of Yahweh. The Hebrew, "house" (baît) denotes a "dwelling" place, and at times "palace," and when in reference to God, it may refer to heavenly dwelling (Dahood 1966, 148). It seems out of place in the context of Psalm 23 to emphasize the presence in the house, but possibly refers to the temple situation where sacrifices are made and communion with Yahweh in feast is commonly understood (Briggs and Briggs 1906, 211). This psalm, perhaps, is a reflection of how God took care of David, as he looked back in his later years. But more, this psalm speaks the heart of a shepherd.

Herbert Lockyer (1983, 73–76) commented that the psalmist, David, effectively utilized the shepherd metaphor to illustrate the providential care of Yahweh to him who listened to his voice and follow his instructions. The Lord as a shepherd is a care-giver, indeed (Ps 23:1). But Yahweh's shepherding responsibility goes beyond care-giving, it also provides rest for our souls, so that we may be refreshed again (Ps 23:2).

In times of need, God graciously restores our souls, and guides us in righteous living (Ps 23:3). Under the shepherding care of God, we should not fear evil and the power of darkness, for Yahweh, our shepherd will protect us. The thought of Yahweh's providential protection comforts us (Ps 23:4) (see Lockyer 1983, 78). God as shepherd is constantly watches over the well-beings of his sheep, and to see that no harm will come upon them (Ps 23:5a). Lockyer described the sheep in a feast filled with dangers from the enemies present at the table, but the presence of the host removed the fear. The host ensures the safety of the guests by being alert and watchful over the banquet (Lockyer 1983, 79).

The preservation of the well-being of the sheep by Yahweh is an extension of his blessings to them (Ps 23:5b). The anointing of oil has healing effect in the shepherding context (Lockyer 1983, 80). This healing power of the oil brings forth blessings to the sheep, and God's blessings are full and abundant and even the flock cannot fully contain them. Finally, David assured us that God's shepherd goodness and love will accompany his people throughout their lives, just as a shepherd showers his goodness and love to his sheep forever.

This is probably due to the experience David had in his earthly life, and therefore, desired to enjoy it eternally (Ps 23:6). It may imply that Yahweh's people; especially leaders, could experience Yahweh's goodness and love if they continued to be in the presence of the shepherd-God. This entire psalm also speaks the shepherding heartbeat of Yahweh as he showered his love and protection over his sheep. This may imply that leadership attitude and approach towards the people, or flock, should be with love, goodness, and to have their welfare constantly in mind.

The context of Psalm 23 juxtaposes the security of the sheep in the presence of the shepherd at the core of the song. David, as a sheep of Yahweh, having enjoyed the leading, protecting, and feeding activities of Yahweh, his shepherd, he anticipated the continuous oversight of Yahweh as their relationship is good. This is supported by the Hebrew, "And I will dwell" (wĕšabttî), where bad relationship does not imply dwelling together. Dahood (1966, 148–149) read it as "eternal happiness in God's celestial abode." This reading may spiritualize its meaning, because the psalmist may simply refer to be with Yahweh, and nothing more. It is best to read as literally, "And I will dwell," just as a sheep dwell in the fold of the shepherd. Here, we see the image of shepherd in leading, protecting, and feeding is best expressed in this psalm of David.

Another reference relates to shepherd metaphor is Psalm 28:9. In this psalm, Yahweh is the subject and the shepherd. The second person singular pronoun indicates that Yahweh is to "help" (yasă') and "bless" (bērak) the people belong to his "possession" (nāḥălāh). The verse then ends with the typical pastoral tone that Yahweh to be their "shepherd" (rĕ'em) and "lift" (nāśā') the sheep on himself always and forever. This gesture of lifting/carrying may connotes a sense of victory over the enemies (Dahood 1966, 173). But in this case, it is a sense of security in the stronger arms, and in this psalm, the sheep is secured in the strong arm of the shepherd. Therefore, we see that the metaphor of shepherd suggests the lifting the sheep as protection.

The concept of God as shepherd is closely related to the lives of Israelites. Psalm 28:9 (NIV) says, "Save your people and bless your inheritance; be their shepherd and carry them forever." Keil and Delitzsch explained that the situation here is where the national life of Israel is at stake, and Yahweh will restore the nation of Israel in the future. Yahweh will lead Israel, like David did, through their predicament (Keil and Delitzch 1986, 366). This portrays the re sponsibility of the shepherd toward the sheep. Clearly, David was commissioned to provide for Israel's needs and blessings. Taking reference from this fashion, the shepherd is one who provides for the flock's needs and protects them from harm, and that is the act of blessing.

The context of the verse 9 of Psalm 28 explains the absence of the reference to the king as shepherd. Briggs and Briggs (1906, 249) suggested that the long period without a monarch in Israel made Yahweh to be the king, naturally, even though referred to as shepherd. But this does not align with the attribution to David as indicated in the headlines, "Of David" (NIV). If this is correct, this psalm was written during the reign of David. What we see in Psalm 28:9 is the Davidic quest for shepherding leadership from Yahweh to lead Israel out of their calamity. It is not that David is incapable to lead, but rather he has faith in the Yahweh, the great Shepherd, that he will deliver his people from the enemies, and bless them. This entails kingship as the image of shepherd.

An aspect of shepherd image is disturbing. The metaphor of shepherd is used to secure the sheep, but at the same time, to slaughter the sheep. In Psalm 49:15 (14 NIV), "death" (māwet) will "shepherd" (yir'ēm) the people (Briggs and Briggs 1906, 410). In the metaphor of shepherd, leading and feeding are part of the shepherd's responsibility, so in this case, death leads the sheep to grave, and destroy their forms (Dahood 1966, 301). The word "mansions" (NIV) is translated from the "exalted dwelling" (zĕbul) equivalent to that of God. Thus, this verse shows that the metaphor can be used in different context to mean differently, and with the same function to produce contrasting results.

The picture of shepherding given in Psalm 78:71–72 is that the shepherd has intimate relationship with the sheep. Briggs and Briggs (1906, 191) commented that the young ones, differ from the regular flock, need special care, so that no harm may come to them. The context given in verse 70 is the restoration of the Davidic dynasty, "He chose David his servant," because this psalm was written by Asaph, "A maskil of Asaph" (NIV). In this case, the psalmist declares that Yahweh will restore the kingdom of Israel under the rulership similar to that of David, who will rule with integrity and guide with aptitude (see Briggs and Briggs 1906, 191–192). In other words, Israel will again be under capable leadership to lead them, and restore them to their former glory.

The shepherd image here emphasizes on the character, rather than the task. Integrity becomes the mantle in governing the people, and aptitude becomes a necessity in guidance. Thus, it is not simply to appoint a shepherd, but find someone who possesses integrity and aptitude in order to rule well.

Psalm 80:2 [1 NIV] is one of the references that infer the title "Shepherd of Israel" (rō'ēh yiśrā'ēl) to Yahweh (Briggs and Briggs 1906, 203). Here Yahweh is portrayed as the shepherd "leading" (nōhēg) Joseph, depicts the relationship between Yahweh and Joseph (see Dahood 1968, 255). Therefore, the title "shepherd of Yahweh" is used of Yahweh, particularly in relation to his people as sheep.

To summarize, the metaphor of shepherd in psalms mainly infer to Yahweh in the image of leading, protecting, and feeding, but leading as the most prominent. Only in Psalm 49:14 (NIV), the metaphor of shepherd is inferred to "death," a negative picture of leading. The other references indicate shepherding in provisions and blessings. In any case, we see that the metaphor of shepherd in Psalms expressed in leading, protecting, and feeding, mainly attributed to Yahweh himself. Next, we shall observe the image of shepherd exhibited in the wisdom literature in the writings of the Hebrew Bible.

Wisdom Literature

The records of wisdom writings are not for head knowledge, but to remind the people of Israel that God is real in their lives. The catch of this truth is the famous philosophical statement, "The fear of the Lord is the beginning of knowledge" (Pr 1:7 NIV).[1] However, wisdom writings do not contain direct or specific references to the shepherd image. The lack of specific reference to shepherd image in the wisdom literature does not rule out its existence in such literary works. We must read in the perspective of the metaphor described in the psalms and other literature of the Hebrew Bible with the relationship between Yahweh as Shepherd and Israel, his sheep. For example, in Psalm 100:3 (NIV), the people of Israel were described as "the sheep of his pasture." In Isaiah 53:6, the sheep was described with the propensity to go astray and being folly. They "have strayed like a lost sheep" (Ps 119:176 NIV) and vulnerable (Ps 44:22 NIV).[2] As sheep, Israel was subject to the anger of her shepherd, Yahweh (Ps 74:1 NIV). But God led Israel as sheep and they were subject to his protection (Ps 78:52–53 NIV).

The wisdom literature formed part of the revelation of Yahweh is also an expression of biblical humanism. This particular type of literature embraced a humanistic perspective of theology, yet not human-centered. Biblical theology of shepherd image derives from the wisdom literature portrays a vivid picture of the relationship between Yahweh the shepherd and Israel the sheep. The shepherding responsibility is to provide and protect for the flock's well-being, and that sets the mandate for pastoral practices in the discipline of pastoral theology, or practical theology. Therefore, the wisdom literature expresses the shepherd image of leading, protecting, and feeding in its theological framework.

The wisdom literature provides wise advices a shepherd needs in leading his sheep. Regarding this, we could relate to Psalm 78:71–72, where we have discovered that shepherd must lead in integrity and aptitude. This may come from the wisdom contained in the wisdom literature. There are more could be said about the relation between wisdom and shepherd metaphor, but we shall summarize in Proverbs 2:6-8 (NIV),

> For the LORD gives wisdom, and from his mouth come knowledge
> and understanding. He holds victory in store for the upright, he is a
> shield to those whose walk is blameless, for he guards the course of
> the just and protects the way of his faithful ones.

This falls in line with the shepherd image observed in the earlier chapters that
the shepherd must lead with knowledge and wisdom that which comes from
Yahweh. Here is a cross reference to the presentation of the shepherd in other
parts of the Hebrew Bible.

There are other references, not to the shepherd metaphor, but to the verb
"rāʿāh," the basic root word of shepherd. These references present different facets of the word but affirm the meanings determined in our study of shepherd
image. In Proverbs 10:21 (NIV), "rāʿāh" is meant "nourish" in the context
where the words come from the righteous or wise will benefit many people, and
on the contrary, the wicked or fool will die in foolishness. In Proverbs 15:14
(NIV), "rāʿāh" is meant "feeds" in the context where the fool will be consumed
by foolishness. These references established that the verb "rāʿāh" is used in the
same meaning as in the shepherd metaphor presented by literature of the Hebrew
Bible.

Indeed, the metaphor of shepherd exists in the wisdom literature implicitly.
Next, we shall observe the image of shepherd in the historical narratives of the
Chronicles.

Chronicles

Unlike wisdom literature, there are direct references to the shepherd image
in the narratives of Chronicles. The text of 1 Chronicles 11:2 (NIV) vividly inferred to David, "You will shepherd of my people Israel." Here, the shepherd
image may express the traits of the metaphor mentioned in Psalm 78:71–72; one
who rules with integrity and guide with aptitude. It is not necessary the one who
is on the throne will exhibit the shepherd image. David was not yet king of Israel
in the context of 1 Chronicles 11:2, but he was recognized as shepherd-king over
the people of Israel as indicated by inference. Therefore, in David, the ideal king
is manifested, and the anointing affirmed the choice of Yahweh to a shepherd
who is knowledgeable and skillful (Hill 2003, 199).

Selman (1994, 1:139) pointed out that the shepherd-king image draws us
back to an ancient meaning that may have special interest in Yahweh's perspective. He stated that the special interest of the shepherd-king image is connected
to the ideal shepherd in the future. This shepherd resembles a king like David.

The Davidic–like king comes in two forms. First, the shepherd image has a
military connotation. David, though a king, is also a mighty warrior. Second, the
relationship between the ideal shepherd and the sheep is sealed with a covenant
(1 Ch 11:3). The anointing of David as king was administered in the presence

of Yahweh, so that Yahweh will be the witness to this relationship.

The shepherd image is not simply one of power and status. It is a covenant relationship, and that has the responsibility and accountability to Yahweh who gave the commission. Therefore, it expresses the activity of leading in the metaphor of shepherd.

The last reference of the metaphor of shepherd in the writings of the Hebrew Bible, 2 Chronicles 18:16, portrays the devastation of Israel without a shepherd. The shepherd is commissioned by Yahweh to lead the people of Israel, as direct assignment from the great shepherd (see 1 Ch 17:6). But the picture in 2 Chronicles 18:16, Israel was in devastation due to the lack of a shepherd (kaṣṣō'n 'ăšer 'ēyn lāhen rō'eh). This tragic imagery is no surprise in prophetic literature, as we have observed earlier. However, Selman (1994, 2:411) perceived this as an opportune time to introduce the pathway leading to the good shepherd. The sheep without a shepherd is lost sheep, and may expose to danger and harm from other wild animals. The only way to be safe is to return to the great Shepherd, Yahweh, so that they will have direction, will be fed, and protected. Other references that indicate sheep without shepherd are Numbers 27:16–17, Isaiah 13:14, Zechariah 10:2, and 13:7.

The remedy to the tragedy caused by the foolish king Ahab could only be found in Yahweh, the good shepherd, or at best, the ideal shepherd to come (see 2 Ch 18). To proclaim peace when the "master" (NIV, 'ādôn) is gone denotes a false proclamation and ridiculous. Micaiah tells the truth of the destruction of the forthcoming battle, and warn to let the people return to their home. It is perhaps, to also mean, return to Yahweh. Micaiah, though a prophet, has shepherding responsibility to lead the people of Israel to their fold, and that direction could only be found in Yahweh. Thus, we see that the image of shepherd stands importantly in the writings of the Hebrew Bible, and in the history of Israel. This is the prominent leading activity of the shepherd metaphor expressed in the leadership of Yahweh, Moses, Israelite leaders, and kings of Israel.

The shepherd metaphor is exhibited in the activities of leading, protecting, and feeding in the writings of the Hebrew Bible. It is undeniably that the image stems from Yahweh, and transmitted to various Israelite leaders and kings. This metaphor presents us a lens to understand the imagery in the Hebrew literature. In so doing, the writings of the Hebrew Bible can be interpreted accurately and appropriately.

To summarize, the metaphor of shepherd, though interspersed in the historical narratives of Chronicles, exhibits in the form of leading in David, the king. This activity forms part of the image of shepherd, with the others as protecting and feeding.

We have concluded our studies of the image of shepherd in the Hebrew Bible, through the Torah, the Prophets, and the Writings. Yet, this knowledge of the shepherd image is closely related to biblical studies, and to which now turn.

Notes

1. Pr 1:7 is parallel by Job 28:28; Ps 111:10; Pr 9:10 and 15:33; see Ecc 12:13–14.

2. See Jer 50:6 (RSV), "lost sheep"; see Jer 23:1 (NIV), "scattering."

CHAPTER EIGHT

THE METAPHOR OF SHEPHERD
AND BIBLICAL STUDIES

The study of the metaphor of shepherd is critical to the understanding of Yahweh and his relationship with his people, the Israelites. This book attempts to garner all meanings, possibly, and that the shepherd metaphor may find its place in biblical studies. In this chapter, the relationship between the metaphor of shepherd and biblical studies will be dealt.

With the significant emphasis of leadership in the shepherd metaphor, there are three implications to biblical studies. First, the shepherd metaphor elucidates the responsibilities of the kings and rulers, as shepherds to their flocks in the study of the Hebrew Bible. The leadership of shepherd provides safety against wild animals and protection from harm to the flock, so the kings and rulers provide safety against enemies and protection from adversaries from the surrounding nations. This image supplements the exegetical process in that the rationale for which the kings and rulers were held responsible to the destruction of the nation is elicited in the context. They are responsible for the well-being of their people, as Yahweh is responsible for the well-beings of his people, Israelites.

Second, the shepherd metaphor exhibits the relationship between the leader and deity, as in relation to the welfare of the people under his leadership, especially in the context of the Hebrew Bible. The Bible contains narratives of ancient times, and to understand them, we must enter into the ancient world. But the cultures of the ancient and contemporary society remain a gulf to be bridged.

The shepherd metaphor, however, fills this gap in two ways. First, it exhibits the relationship between the deity and the leader of the biblical world in that the people are required to respect leadership. Throughout ancient history, kings were perceived as leaders of the nation and commanded orders to be performed. This perception is explicated as we observed the shepherd metaphor represented the deity on earth to rule and lead the nation, of which the concept of territorial deities is common in the ancient world. Second, it exhibits the responsibility of the leader to the people in that, as divine representation the leader is responsible to the needs, such as food and protection, of the people. The victory of the nation reflects the strength and the defeat expressed the weakness of the leader, as well as the deity, which is a prominent concept in the ancient world. Thus, the understanding of the shepherd metaphor bridges the cultural gap by exhibiting the vested authority from the deity over the people, and in relation to the welfare of the people.

Third, the shepherd metaphor provides a perspective to exegesis. Biblical exegesis requires various reading pattern to explore the literature of the Bible. The undeniable fact is that apart from the exegetical methods, a presupposition underlies in the reading of the Bible. This presupposition provides a framework to interpret the biblical text by employing the critical methods with the perspective of its stance. With the understanding of the shepherd metaphor exhibited in the Hebrew Bible, as explicated earlier, Yahweh is shepherd and Israel is his flock. This relationship provides a perspective to interpret the Hebrew Bible. Utilizing the perspective of shepherding, Yahweh is perceived as the shepherd who leads Israel through their life journey, feeds them when they are in need, and protects them when they are in danger. It permeates into the literary expressions in history, prophecy, poetry, and wisdom literature, by displaying the connection of these various expressions in the relationship between Yahweh and Israel, as shepherd and flock. For example, the provision of the Messiah is perceived as part of the perspective of shepherding, because Yahweh is the shepherd of Israel and he will provide the redemptive plan to his people. Reading from this perspective helps us to understand the rationale behind the actions of Yahweh in history and to correlate the historical events to the acts of Yahweh that are interspersed in the Hebrew Bible. The end result may illuminate the unity of these sacred pages hidden in the literary treasure.

In summary, the metaphor of shepherd is not simply a metaphorical device utilized by biblical writers, but it provides a crucial perspective to biblical exegesis. This image of shepherding perceives the biblical literature from the perspective of the relationship of Yahweh and Israel. On the same token, this perspective of shepherding is useful in reading the New Testament and to understand the continuation of Yahweh's designed purpose, beginning with Israel and to the world.

CONCLUSION

The metaphor of shepherd is prominent in the literature of the ancient Near East and Hebrew Bible. It is a common usage in the culture of ancient Near East to refer to the kings and rulers as shepherd, and the people as sheep. As part of that culture, Israel is familiar with this appellation in reference to their rulers and kings.

The metaphor of shepherd in the Hebrew Bible sets stage for a biblical theology of shepherding with an emphasis of leadership in contrast to the therapeutic image exhibited in the contemporary pastoral theology. It builds on the biblical foundations of Yahweh as shepherd, as well as the other leaders and kings of Israel. This image is profoundly embracing the activities of leading, protecting, and feeding, in the roles of king, priest, and prophet. Therefore, the theology of shepherding derived from the metaphor of shepherd should be the foundation of the formulation of pastoral theology.

The exploration of shepherd metaphor, though not exhaustive, can also lead to further development in biblical studies in relation to Yahweh as shepherd and other Israelite leaderships, as well as in-depths study of the various shepherding activities in the narratives of the Hebrew Bible, and the Greek New Testament. However, one can be confident that the Hebrew Bible contains the ideology of shepherding either equal or more substantial than the New Testament. What needs emphasis is that the Hebrew Bible is the foundation of the New Testament. The study of shepherd image must begin from the materials of the Hebrew Bible, and proceed progressively to the New Testament in order to grasp the significance of being a shepherd.

The study of the shepherd metaphor is based on historical-literary exegesis, and it must not be taken lightly. Metaphorical language is placed side by side with the historical knowledge of the text. Grammar, syntax, and semantics of the Hebrew language must be read in the light of the political, social, and religious aspects of the culture of ancient Israel. It is infused with historical and literary skills. The study of metaphor in the historical-literary exegesis will lead to understand the imagery in its historical setting. However, there may be exegetical issues that have not been dealt with thoroughly, or perhaps waiting to be discovered. What is evident here pertaining to the metaphor of shepherd in the Hebrew Bible has been consolidated. The trend to develop the shepherding metaphor in doing exegesis is yet new and raw. In all these, we learn how Yahweh is to his people, Israel a shepherd, and who are they as sheep to him. The relationship of shepherd and sheep ties Yahweh and Israel together, and if derail from this relationship, the course of future for his people is detrimental.

BIBLIOGRAPHY

Adams, Jay E. 1979. *Shepherding God's Flock*. Grand Rapids: Baker.

Allen, Leslie C. 1990. *Ezekiel 20–48*. Word Biblical Commentary. Vol. 29. Dallas: Word Books, Publishers.

Anderson, A. A. 1989. *2 Samuel*. Word Biblical Commentary. Vol. 11. Dallas: Word Books, Publishers.

Andersen, Francis I. and David N. Freedman. 1980. *Hosea*. The Anchor Bible. New York: Doubleday.

_____. 1989. *Amos*. The Anchor Bible. New York: Doubleday.

_____. 2000. *Micah*. The Anchor Bible. New York: Doubleday.

Anderson, Ray S. 1979. "A Theology for Ministry." *Theological Foundations for Ministry*. Ed. Ray S. Anderson. Grand Rapids: Eerdmans and Edinburgh: T & T Clark, Ltd.

Baldwin, Joyce G. 1988. *1 and 2 Samuel*. The Tyndale Old Testament Commentaries. Ed. D. J. Wiseman. Illinois: Inter-Varsity Press.

Barton, John. 1996. *Reading the Old Testament: Method in Biblical Study*. Revised and Enlarged. Louisville: Westminster John Knox Press.

Beyreuther, E. 1978. "Shepherd." *The New International Dictionary of New Testament Theology*. Vol. 3. Ed. Colin Brown. Exeter: Paternoster Press.

Bushell, Michael S. and Michael D. Tan. 1998. *BibleWorks for Windows*. CD-ROM. Window 95/NT Release 4.0.035p. Minnesota: BibleWorks, LLC and

104   BIBLIOGRAPHY

HERMENEUTIKA Computer Bible Research Software.

Brettler, Marc Zvi. 1989. *God is King: understanding an Israelite metaphor.* Journal for the Study of the Old Testament, Supplement series 76. Sheffield: Sheffield Academic Press.

Briggs, Charles A. and Emilie G. Briggs. 1906. *A Critical and Exegetical Commentary on the Book of Psalms.* The International Critical Commentary. Edinburgh: T. & T. Clark.

Bright, John. 1965. *Jeremiah.* The Anchor Bible. New York: Doubleday.

Brueggemann, Walter. 1979. "Covenanting as Human Vocation." *Interpretation* 33: 115–129.

Budd, Philip J. 1984. *Numbers.* Word Biblical Commentary. Vol. 5. Nashville: Thomas Nelson Publishers.

Bullock, C. Hassell. 1986. *An Introduction to the Old Testament Prophetic Books.* Chicago: Moody.

Childs, Brevard S. 1970. *Biblical Theology in Crisis.* Philadelphia: Westminster Press.

_____. 1979. *Introduction to the Old Testament as Scripture.* Philadelphia: Fortress Press.

_____. 1985. *Old Testament Theology in a Canonical Context.* Philadelphia: Fortress Press.

Clebsch, William A. and Charles R. Jaekle. 1964. *Pastoral Care in Historical Perspective.* New Jersey: Prentice-Hall.

Cooke, G. A. 1936. *A Critical and Exegetical Commentary on the Book of Ezekiel.* The International Critical Commentary. Edinburgh: T. & T. Clark.

Dahood, S. J., Mitchell. 1966. *Psalms I: 1–50.* The Anchor Bible. New York: Doubleday.

_____. 1968. *Psalms II: 51–100.* The Anchor Bible. New York: Doubleday.

Delitzsch, Franz. 1969. *Biblical Commentary on the Prophecies of Isaiah.* Vol. II. Trans. James Martin. Grand Rapids: Eerdmans.

DeVries, Simon J. 1985. *1 Kings.* Word Biblical Commentary. Vol. 12. Waco: Word Books.

Eichrodt, Walther. 1961. *Theology of the Old Testament.* Vol. 1. Philadelphia: Westminster Press.

Elliger, K. and W. Rudolph, eds. 1967–1977. *Biblia Hebraica Stuttgartensia.* Stuttgart:

Deutsche Bibelgesellschaft.

Enns, Peter. 2000. *Exodus*. The NIV Application Commentary. Grand Rapids: Zondervan.

Finley, Thomas J. 1990. *Joel, Amos, Obadiah*. The Wycliffe Exegetical Commentary. Ed. Kenneth Baker. Chicago: Moody Press.

Fisher, David. 1996. *The 21ˢᵗ Century Pastor*. Grand Rapids: Zondervan.

Friedman, Richard Elliot. 2001. *Commentary on the Torah*. New York: HarperCollins Publishers.

Gardiner, Alan. 1957. *Egyptian Grammar*. Third Revised Edition. Oxford: Griffith Institute, Ashmolean Museum.

Goldsworthy, Graeme L. 1981. *Gospel and Kingdom: A Christian Interpretation of the Old Testament*. Carlisle: Paternoster Press.

_____. 1991. *According to Plan: The Unfolding Revelation of God in the Bible*. Leicester: Inter-varsity Press.

Hamilton, Victor P. 1990. *The Books of Genesis Chapters 1–17*. The New International Commentary on the Old Testament. Grand Rapids: Eerdmans.

Hill, Andrew E. 2003. *1 and 2 Chronicles. The NIV Application Commentary*. Grand Rapids: Zondervan.

Hiltner, Seward. 1958. *Preface to Pastoral Theology*. Nashville: Abingdon Press.

Holladay, William L., ed. 1971. *A Concise Hebrew and Aramaic Lexicon of the Old Testament*. Grand Rapids: Eerdmans and Leiden: E.J. Brill.

Holladay, William L. 1989. *A Commentary on the Book of the Prophet Jeremiah Chapters 26–52*. Hermeneia. Mineapolis: Fortress Press.

Jacob, Edmund. 1958. *Theology of the Old Testament*. New York: Harper & Brothers Publishers.

Kautzsch, E. 1910. *Gesenius' Hebrew Grammar*. Second English Edition. Trans. A. E. Cowley. Oxford: Clarendon Press.

Keil, C. F. and F. Delitzch. 1986. *Commentary on the Old Testament*. 10 Vols. Grand Rapids: Eerdmans.

_____. 1986a. "The Pentateuch." *The Commentary on the Old Testament*. Trans. James Martin. Grand Rapids: Eerdmans.

_____. 1986b. "Psalms." *Old Testament Commentaries*. Trans. M. G. Easton. Grand

Rapids: Eerdmans.

Langdon, Stephen. 1931. "The Legend of Etana and the Eagle." *Babyloniaca*. Vol. 12: 1–53.

LaSor, William S.; David A. Hubbard and Frederic W. Bush. 1982. *Old Testament Survey*. Grand Rapids: Eerdmans.

Levine, Baruch A. 2000. *Numbers 21-36*. The Anchor Bible. New York: Doubleday.

Lisowsky, Gerhard. 1958. *Konkordanz zum Hebraischen Alten Testament*. Stuttgart: Deutsche Bibelgesellschaft.

Lockyer, Herbert. 1983. *God's Book of Poetry*. Nashville: Nelson.

Macintosh, A. H. 1997. *A Critical and Exegetical Commentary on Hosea*. The International Critical Commentary. Edinburgh: T. & T. Clark.

McCarter, P. Kyle Jr. 1984. *2 Samuel*. The Anchor Bible Commentary. New York: Doubleday.

McComiskey, Thomas E. 1992. "Hosea." *The Minor Prophets:An Exegetical & expository Commentary*. Vol. 1. Ed. Thomas E. McComiskey. Grand Rapids: Baker.

_____. 1998. "Zechariah." *The Minor Prophets: An Exegetical & Expository Copmmentary*. Vol. 3. Ed. Thomas E. McComiskey. Grand Rapids: Baker.

McKane, William. 1986. *A Critical and Exegetical on Jeremiah*. The International Critical Commentary. 2 Vols. Edinburgh: T. & T. Clark Ltd.

McKenzie, John L. 1968. *Second Isaiah*. The Anchor Bible. New York: Doubleday.

Meyer, von E. 1906. *Die Israeliten und ihre Nachbarstamme*. INS. mit Beitragen van B. Luther.

Milgrom, Jacob. 1989. *Numbers*. The JPS Torah Commentary. Philadelphia: The Jewish Publication Society.

Mitchell, Hinckly G. 1912. *A Critical and Exegetical Commentary on Haggai and Zechariah*. The International Critical Commentary. Edinburgh: T. & T. Clark.

Motyer, J. Alec. 1993. *The Prophecy of Isaiah*. Illinois: InterVarsity Press.

Neighbors, Ralph. 1990. *Where Do We Go From Here*? Singapore: Touch Publications, Inc.

Niehaus, Jeffrey. 1992. "Amos." *The minor Prophets*. Vol. 1. Ed. Thomas E. McComiskey. Grand Rapids: Baker.

Oden, Thomas C. 1983. *Pastoral Theology*. San Francisco: Harper & Row, Publishers.

Pattern, Richard D. 1991. *Nahum, Habakkuk, Zephaniah*. The Wycliffe Exegetical Commentary. Ed. Kenneth Baker. Chicago: Moody Press.

Plaut, W. Gunther. 1981. *The Torah*. A Modern Commentary. New York: Union of American Hebrew Congregations.

Pritchard, James B., ed. 1969. *Ancient Near Eastern Texts Relating to the Old Testament*. Third edition. Princeton: Princeton University Press.

Propp, William H. C. 1999. *Exodus 1-18*. The Anchor Bible. New York: Doubleday.

von Rad, Gerhard. 1975. *Old Testament Theology*. Vol. 1. London: SCM Press.

Ross, Allen. 1985. "Psalms." *The Bible Knowledge Commentary*. Eds. John F. Walvoord and Roy B. Zuck. Illinois: Victor.

Russell, Anthony. 1980. *The Clerical Profession*. London: SPCK.

Sailhamer, John H. 1995. *Introduction to Old Testament Theology: A Canonical Approach*. Grand Rapids: Zondervan.

_____. 1998. *Genesis*. The Expositor's Bible Commentary. Ed. Frank E. Gaebelein. CD-ROM. Grand Rapids: Zondervan.

Sarna, Nahum M. 1989. *Genesis*. The JPS Torah Commentary. Philadelphia: The Jewish Publication Society.

Schafer, Heinrich. 1905. *Urkunden der Alteren Athiopenkonige*. Leipzig: J.C. Hinrichs'sche Buchhandlung.

Schmidt, L. 1970. *Menschlicher Erfolg und Jahwes Initiative*. Studien zu Tradition, Interpretation und Historie in Uberlieferungen von Gideon, Saul, und David. Wissenschaftliche Monographien zum Alten und Neuen Testament 38. Neukirchen-Vluyn: Neukirchener Verlag.

Selman, Martin J. 1994. *1 Chronicles*. Tyndale Old Testament Commentaries. Illinois: Inter-Varsity Press.

_____. 1994a. *2 Chronicles*. Tyndale Old Testament Commentaries. Illinois: Inter-Varsity Press.

Shedd, William G. T. 1965. *Homiletics and Pastoral Theology*. London: Banner of Truth.

Skinner, John. 1930. *A Critical and Exegetical Commentary on Genesis*. The International Critical Commentary. Second Edition. Edinburgh: T. & T. Clark.

Smith, John Merlin Pouis. 1911. *A Critical and Exegetical Commentary on the Books of*

Micah, Zephaniah and Nahum. The International Critical Commentary. Edinburgh: T. & T. Clark.

Speiser, E. A. 1964. *Genesis. The Anchor Bible.* New York: Doubleday.

Strom, Mark. 1990. *The Symphony of Scripture.* Illinois: Intervarsity Press.

Stuart, Douglas. 1987. *Hosea-Jonah.* Vol. 31. Word Biblical Commentary. Texas: Word Books.

Sunderland, R. S., ed. 1981. *A Biblical Basis for Ministry.* Philadelphia: Westminster.

Thiessen, John C. 1962. *Pastoring the Smaller Church.* Grand Rapids: Zondervan.

Thornton, Martin. 1956. *Pastoral Theology: A Reorientation.* London: SPCK.

_____. 1968. *The Function of Theology.* London: Hodder & Stoughton.

Tidball, Derek. 1986. *Skilful Shepherds.* Grand Rapids: Zondervan.

Vos, Geerhardus. 1975. *Biblical Theology: Old and New Testaments.* Edinburgh: The Banner of Truth.

Waltke, Bruce K. 1993. "Micah." *The Minor Prophets.* Vol. 2. Ed. Thomas E. McComiskey. Grand Rapids: Baker.

Watts, John D. W. 1987. *Isaiah 34-66. Word Biblical Commentary.* Vol. 25. Waco: Word Books, Publisher.

Wenham, Gordon J. 1987. *Genesis 1-15. Word Biblical Commentary.* Vol. 1. Waco: Word Books, Publishers.

Wolf, Herbert. 1991. *An Introduction to the Old Testament Pentateuch.* Chicago: Moody.

Wolff, Hans W. 1974. *A Commentary on the Book of the Prophet Hosea.* Hermeneia. Philadelphia: Fortress Press.

Zimmerli, Walther. 1907. *Old Testament Theology in Outline.* Trans. David E. Green. Altanta: John Knox

SCRIPTURE INDEX

SUBJECT INDEX